The
A-Z of Property
Terms

Specialist dictionaries

Dictionary of Accounting	0 7475 6991 6
Dictionary of Agriculture	0 7136 7778 3
Dictionary of Banking and Finance	0 7136 7739 2
Dictionary of Business	0 7136 7918 2
Dictionary of Computing	0 7475 6622 4
Dictionary of Economics	0 7136 8203 5
Dictionary of Environment and Ecology	0 7475 7201 1
Dictionary of Food Science and Nutrition	0 7136 7784 8
Dictionary of Human Resources and Personnel Management	0 7136 8142 X
Dictionary of Information and Library Management	0 7136 7591 8
Dictionary of Leisure, Travel and Tourism	0 7475 7222 4
Dictionary of Media Studies	0 7136 7593 4
Dictionary of Medical Terms	0 7136 7603 5
Dictionary of Nursing	0 7475 6634 8
Dictionary of Politics and Government	0 7475 7220 8
Dictionary of Publishing and Printing	0 7136 7589 6
Dictionary of Science and Technology	0 7475 6620 8
Dictionary of Sports Science	0 7136 7785 6

Easier English™ titles

Easier English Basic Dictionary	0 7475 6644 5
Easier English Basic Synonyms	0 7475 6979 7
Easier English Dictionary: Handy Pocket Edition	0 7475 6625 9
Easier English Intermediate Dictionary	0 7475 6989 4
Easier English Student Dictionary	0 7475 6624 0
English Thesaurus for Students	1 9016 5931 3

Check Your English Vocabulary workbooks

Academic English	0 7475 6691 7
Business	0 7475 6626 7
Human Resources	0 7475 6997 5
Living in the UK	0 7136 7914 X
Medicine	0 7136 7590 X
FCE +	0 7475 6981 9
IELTS	0 7136 7604 3
PET	0 7475 6627 5
Phrasal Verbs and Idioms	0 7136 7805 4
TOEFL®	0 7475 6984 3
TOEIC	0 7136 7508 X

Visit our website for full details of all our books: **www.acblack.com**

The
A-Z of Property
Terms

www.acblack.com

First published in Great Britain in 2006

A & C Black Publishers Ltd
38 Soho Square, London W1D 3HB

A CIP record for this book is available from the British Library

ISBN-10: 0 7136 7783 X
ISBN-13: 978 0 7136 7783 6

Text Production and Proofreading
Heather Bateman, Katy McAdam, Howard Sargeant, Lauren Simpson

This book is produced using paper that is made from wood grown in managed,
sustainable forests. It is natural, renewable and recyclable. The logging and
manufacturing processes conform to the environmental regulations of the country
of origin.

Text typeset by A & C Black
Printed and bound in Great Britain by Bookmarque Ltd, Croydon, Surrey

Introduction

Ask anyone who has ever bought, sold, let or renovated a property about their experiences, and they'll probably tell you that it can be a time-consuming, daunting and downright confusing business.

At such a potentially stressful time as buying or selling a home, one of the most frustrating tasks is getting to grips with the endless technical jargon. Even old hands at the process can sometimes find themselves struggling to make sense of what their estate agent, surveyor, builder or financial advisor is talking about.

Whether you need to decipher a surveyor's report or a mortgage document, the A-Z of Property Terms has been expertly compiled to help you cut straight through the confusion. Containing over 3,000 key words and phrases, it is ideal for first-time buyers and sellers, tenants, landlords, developers, tradespersons, builders and buy-to-let investors.

Whatever type of transaction you're involved in, the A-Z of Property Terms is the ultimate jargon-busting glossary. We hope that it proves invaluable as you negotiate the property maze.

Our thanks go to Victoria Young, Martin Sandall and Julie Steele for their valuable help and advice during the making of this book.

A

abandonment (of easement) *noun* an agreement to give up a right to use a part of another person's property, e.g. a common access route

Abatement Notice *noun* a legal order to stop doing something which is creating a statutory nuisance, such as smoke or noise pollution, served under the 1990 Environmental Protection Act

abatement procedure *noun* the act of stopping someone from creating an environmental nuisance, by serving an Abatement Notice on them

abeyance *noun* a condition in which legal ownership of an estate has not been established

ABI *abbreviation* Association of British Insurers

abogado, abogada *noun* (*in Spain*) a lawyer

Abolition of Feudal Tenure etc (Scotland) Act 2000 *noun* an act that replaced the feudal system of land ownership that had existed in Scotland with a system of outright ownership of land

absolute title *noun* land registered with the Land Registry, in which case the owner has a guaranteed title to the land (NOTE: Absolute title also exists to leasehold land, giving the proprietor a guaranteed valid lease.)

abstract of title *noun* a summary of the details of the ownership of a property that has not been registered

abutment *noun* **1.** the state of touching or being adjacent to an object or piece of land along one side **2.** the point at which two things abut **3.** a structure that supports or bears the thrust of something

abuttal *noun* the boundaries of a piece of land in relation to land that is adjoining

accelerated possession procedure *noun* a legal procedure that allows a landlord's claim to repossess a property at the end of a tenancy to be decided by a court purely on the basis of written representations

acceptance *noun* **1.** a written or verbal indication that someone agrees to an invitation or offer **2.** formal written or verbal agreement showing that someone assents to the terms and conditions in a contract

access *noun* a means of entering or approaching a place, e.g. a door or a driveway ■ *verb* to find a means of entering or approaching a place

accessibility *noun* how easy it is to enter or approach a place, e.g. for a wheelchair user

accessible *adjective* easy to enter or approach, e.g. for a wheelchair user

Access to Neighbouring Land Act *noun* an act that gives a right of access to a neighbour's land in order to carry out basic preservation works on your own property

accident, sickness and unemployment insurance *noun* insurance cover that protects against loss of income in cases of accident, illness or unemployment

accident policy *noun* any insurance policy that pays money if an accident takes place (NOTE: Accident policies can be held by employers to cover claims made by employees, by companies to cover claims made by the public, or by an individual against personal financial loss.)

accompanied viewing *noun* a service for sellers of property in which an estate agent conducts a viewing of the property for prospective buyers

accrued interest *noun* interest that has been earned by an interest-bearing investment

ACH *abbreviation* Automated Clearing House

ACOP *abbreviation* Approved Code of Practice

acoustic engineer *noun* an engineer who gives advice on reducing unwanted noise in a building, usually at the design stage

acoustic panel *noun* a panel of soundproof material that fits together with others to form a soundproof surface, e.g. a wall or ceiling

acoustics *noun* the study of sound, especially noise levels in buildings ■ *plural noun* the quality of the sound in a room, affected by the shape and size of the room and the materials used in it

acre *noun* a unit of area used in some countries, including the United States and the United Kingdom, equal to 4,046.86 sq. m./4,840 sq. yd

acte de vente *noun* (*in France*) a deed of sale, usually drawn up by a notary

actual occupation *noun* a person who is living in a property at the present time

actual possession *noun* the situation of occupying and controlling land and buildings

addendum *noun* something that is or has been added, e.g. to a contract

additional loan *noun* a second or subsequent loan to a mortgage holder at one of the mortgage rates that the lender is offering its customers

additional principal payment *noun* a mortgage payment that is higher than the scheduled amount, made in order to reduce both the outstanding loan and the interest on it

additional survey *noun* a detailed survey carried out on a specific aspect of a property, e.g. the condition of the roof or the electrical system, in addition to the main valuation or homebuyer's survey

adjoin *verb* to be next to or share a common border with another property or area of land

adjoining *adjective* next to and touching something else

adjustable rate mortgage *noun* a mortgage in which the interest rate changes according to the current market rates. Abbreviation **ARM**

adjustor *noun* same as **loss adjustor**

administration fee *noun* a fee that lenders charge for providing a mortgage, nominally to cover the cost of sourcing funds and normally non-refundable if the mortgage does not proceed

administrative receiver *noun* a person appointed by a court to administer the affairs of a company

ad valorem duty *noun* a tax calculated according to the value of the goods taxed

advance *noun* **1.** a quantity of money or goods supplied before payment is made or repayments begin **2.** a loan of money ■ *verb* to supply something or part of something, especially money, before it is due

adverse credit *noun* the fact of owing money, especially of having a bad credit history that makes obtaining a mortgage difficult

adverse credit mortgage *noun* a mortgage made available to someone with a bad credit history, usually with a non-mainstream lender

adverse possession *noun* an occupation of property by squatters or others that is contrary to the rights of the real owner

adverse rights *noun* any rights or easements that somebody else has over a property on the market, which could be inconvenient for new owners

Advocate General *noun* **1.** one of the two Law Officers for Scotland **2.** one of eight independent members forming part of the European Court of Justice together with 15 judges, who summarises and presents a case to the judges to assist them in coming to a decision

Advocate General for Scotland *noun* the principal legal adviser on Scots law to the Scottish Executive and the UK government

AER *noun* a way of expressing the interest rate on accounts that can be in credit or in debit, e.g. current accounts, that represents what the annual rate of interest would be if the interest was compounded each time it was paid. Full form **annual equivalent rate**

aerated block *noun* a lightweight building block with excellent insulating properties, made of concrete with a foaming agent added

aerator *noun* a device for putting gas bubbles into a body of water such as a pond, in order to purify it

affordability matrix *noun* **1.** a system for calculating how affordable the housing is in a particular area **2.** a system used by mortgage lenders for calculating whether a prospective borrower can afford mortgage repayments, based on salary and credit information

Affordable Rural Housing Commission *noun* a UK government commission established to identify ways of improving access to affordable housing for people in rural areas. Abbreviation **ARHC**

A-frame building *noun* a style of building that looks, end on, like an inverted letter V, with the surfaces of the sloping roof coming down almost to the ground and forming the external walls

agency *noun* a company that acts as the agent, representative or subcontractor of a person or another company

agency agreement *noun* an agreement that allows one party to sell the goods or products of another party in return for commission payments

agent *noun* **1.** someone who officially represents someone else, e.g. in buying and selling property or insurance **2.** someone who provides a particular service for someone else

agente de fincas *noun* (*in Spain*) an estate agent

agente de propiedad inmobiliaria *noun* (*in Spain*) an estate agent

agente immobiliare *noun* (*in Italy*) an estate agent

Agentes de la Propiedad Inmobiliaria *noun* (*in Spain*) a regulatory body for estate agency. Abbreviation **API** (NOTE: Purchasers of property in Spain should look for API or GIPE accreditation when searching for a reputable estate agent)

agent immobilier *noun* (*in France*) an estate agent

aggregate *noun* broken stone, gravel and sand used in road construction and, when mixed with cement and water, for making concrete

agreed price *noun* the price that has been accepted by both the buyer and seller

agricultural dwelling *noun* a dwelling built in open countryside, away from existing settlements, for which special planning permission is required and rarely granted

agricultural restriction *noun* a rule in the granting of planning permission that restricts occupancy of a dwelling to people engaged in agriculture or horticulture

agricultural waste *noun* waste matter produced on a farm, e.g. plastic containers for pesticides

air brick *noun* a brick that is perforated to allow for ventilation in a building, usually below floor level

aircraft noise *noun* the noise of passing aircraft heard from a property

airlock *noun* an obstruction to the flow of a liquid in a pipe, caused by a bubble of air

air vent *noun* an air brick or other vent set into a wall to provide ventilation in a building

alcove *noun* **1.** a recess in the wall of a room **2.** a recess in an exterior wall, usually with a roof or other covering structure

allodial land *noun* (*in Scotland*) land owned free of any encumbrances, as distinct from feudal property, e.g. church property

allotment *noun* a small plot of publicly owned land rented to a person for growing vegetables or flowers

all-risks insurance *noun* insurance that provides a broad scope of cover, although generally and confusingly does not cover against all and every eventuality

alluvium *noun* the silt deposited by a river or a lake

alteration *noun* a substantial change made to the fabric or function of a building

alteration project *noun* a project to considerably renovate, or change the function of, a building

amenity *noun* **1.** a useful or attractive feature or service, e.g. leisure facilities **2.** the experience of a place as pleasant or attractive

amenity green space *noun* areas of green space used for recreation, including parks and gardens, informal recreation areas and outdoor sports areas

American bond *noun* a style of bricklaying in which every fifth or sixth course of bricks is laid end on, not side on

American Society of Home Inspectors *noun* (*in the US*) the professional body that regulates the certification and licensing of surveyors

amortisation *noun* payment of a debt in a series of instalments

anchor *noun* any device that keeps an object in place

anchor bolt *noun* a heavy-duty bolt fitted into masonry to allow other structural elements to be connected

ancient woodland *noun* a wooded area that has been covered with trees for many hundreds of years

ancillary relief *noun* financial provision or adjustment of property rights ordered by a court for a spouse or child in divorce proceedings

annual equivalent rate *noun* full form of **AER**

annual interest *noun* the amount of interest paid on borrowing over the period of a year

annual percentage rate *noun* full form of **APR**

annuity *noun* **1.** an amount of money paid to someone yearly or at some other regular interval **2.** an investment that pays the investor a fixed amount of money each year for a number of years, often the investor's lifetime

annuity mortgage *noun* ♦ **repayment method**

anodise *verb* to add a coating to metal to protect against corrosion and abrasion

a non domino *phrase* (*in Scottish law*) from someone who is not the owner

a non domino disposition *noun* (*in Scottish law*) a gift of property made by someone who is not the owner of it, unchallengeable after 10 years' possession

anti-climb paint *noun* paint that gives a very rough surface, used on upright structures such as walls and posts for preventing intruders from climbing up them

antisocial behaviour *noun* bad or unpleasant behaviour in public

Antisocial Behaviour Act *noun* a piece of UK legislation the provisions of which address, among others things, the behaviour of neighbours towards each other, in relation, e.g., to noise nuisance

anti-vandal paint *noun* a non-drying paint applied to surfaces to prevent intruders from climbing on them or defacing them

AONB *abbreviation* Area of Outstanding Natural Beauty

APACS *noun* a UK trade association for institutions that provide payment services to customers. Full form **Association for Payment Clearing Services**

apartment *noun* **1.** *US* a flat **2.** a single room in a residential building (*formal*) Abbreviation **apt**

appellant *noun* a person who goes to a higher court to ask it to change a decision or a sentence imposed by a lower court

applicant *noun* **1.** someone who applies for something, e.g. a mortgage **2.** someone who applies for a court order

applicator gun *noun* a tool used for applying flexible sealants stored in tubes

appoint *verb* to choose someone to act as your representative or agent

apportion *verb* to share out something such as property, rights or liabilities in appropriate proportions

apportionment *noun* the act of sharing out something such as property, rights or liabilities in appropriate proportions

appraisal *noun* an estate agent's estimate of how much money a property is worth

appropriate *verb* **1.** to take control of something illegally **2.** to take something for a particular use, e.g. to take funds from an estate to pay legacies to beneficiaries

appropriation *noun* the allocation of money for a particular purpose such as distributing parts of an estate to beneficiaries

approval *noun* formal or official agreement, e.g. to provide a mortgage to a borrower

Approved Code of Practice *noun* an official guideline from the Health and Safety Executive for best practice in construction. Abbreviation **ACOP**

appurtenances *plural noun* land or buildings attached to or belonging to a property

APR *noun* a way of expressing interest on a loan that takes into account the basic interest rate and any other fees and costs charged in relation to the loan. Full form **annual percentage rate**

apron *noun* the projecting edge of a platform such as a theatre stage, dock or porch

apt *abbreviation* apartment

arbitration *noun* the settling of a dispute by an outside person or persons agreed on by both sides

arbour *noun* a shaded place in a garden for sitting in, or a wooden structure used as the basis for creating one, for supporting climbing plants

arch *noun* **1.** a curved structure that forms the upper edge of an open space such as a window, a doorway or the space between a bridge's supports **2.** an entrance or passageway under an arch ■ *verb* to build something in the shape of an arch or with arch-shaped supports

architect *noun* someone whose job is to design buildings and advise on their construction

Architects' Council of Europe *noun* a European organisation that seeks to monitor and influence EU policy in relation to the built environment, with members that include the representative and regulatory bodies of EU and other European countries

Architects' Registration Board *noun* a UK organisation that registers all architects, promotes good practice and deals with complaints

architectural drawing *noun* a two-dimensional illustration showing the features of a proposed architectural design

architecture *noun* **1.** the art and science of designing and constructing buildings **2.** a style or fashion of building, especially one that is typical of a period of history or of a particular place

Architecture and Surveying Institute *noun* a UK teaching and examining body for architects, surveyors and engineers

architrave *noun* a decorative strip of wood or plaster forming a frame around a door or window

Area of Outstanding Natural Beauty *noun* (*in England and Wales*) a region that is not a National Park but is considered sufficiently attractive to be preserved from unsympathetic development. Abbreviation **AONB**

ARHC *abbreviation* Affordable Rural Housing Commission

ARM *abbreviation* adjustable rate mortgage

armoured cable *noun* heavy-duty cable that carries electricity underground or overhead

arquitecto, arquitecta *noun* (*in Spain*) an architect

arrangement fee *noun* a charge made by a bank to a client for arranging credit facilities

arrhes *plural noun* (*in France*) a deposit paid by the purchaser that is forfeited if the purchaser withdraws from the transaction, with double the amount being refunded if the vendor withdraws

Artex a trade name for a surface coating for interior decorating to which a decorator can add any pattern or texture

asbestos *noun* a mineral formerly used in the construction industry to make buildings fire-resistant, now known to cause serious health problems (NOTE: The use of asbestos in construction has been banned in the UK since 1985. However, it is still found in many older buildings and poses serious health risks if dislodged from walls during maintenance or rebuilding work. A thorough survey should be conducted for asbestos in at-risk buildings before any such work is undertaken.)

asbestosis *noun* a disease of the lungs caused by inhaling asbestos dust

ashlar *noun* **1.** a thin slab of squared stone, used for facing walls or in building **2.** masonry using thin slabs of squared stone as facing material

asking price *noun* a price that a seller is asking for the property being sold, which, after negotiation, may be higher or lower than the final sale price

asphalt *noun* **1.** a brownish-black solid or semisolid substance that is a by-product of petroleum distillation, used for surfacing roads and paths and for waterproofing **2.** a surfacing material composed mainly of asphalt and gravel that hardens on cooling and is used for making roads and paths

asset *noun* a property to which a value can be assigned

assign *verb* (*in Scotland*) to transfer ownership of a property or right to another party by signing a document

assignation *noun* (*in Scotland*) the assigning of a property or right; or the written document by which a property or right is assigned

assignee *noun* someone who receives something that has been assigned

assignment *noun* (*in Scotland*) a document such as a deed that effects a legal transfer of rights

assignor *noun* someone who assigns something to someone else

assigns *plural noun* people to whom property has been assigned

assisted move scheme *noun* a scheme under which a developer from whom a client is buying a new house manages the sale of the old house by estate agents and pays the agency fees

Association for Environment Conscious Building *noun* a UK organisation established to facilitate environmentally friendly practices within the construction industry

Association for Payment Clearing Services *noun* full form of **APACS**

Association of British Insurers *noun* an organisation representing British companies that are authorised to carry out insurance business. Abbreviation **ABI**

Association of Building Engineers *noun* a UK organisation established to facilitate cooperation between the various branches of the construction industry

Association of Independent Inventory Clerks *noun* a UK organisation that provides professional inventory services to landlords, tenants and agents

Association of Plumbing and Heating Contractors *noun* a UK trade association for the plumbing and heating industries

Association of Property Bankers *noun* a UK organisation that seeks to foster a better understanding of property finance within the banking and property sectors

Association of Relocation Professionals *noun* a UK trade association for companies and professionals involved in the business of corporate and residential relocation

Association of Residential Letting Agents *noun* a UK professional self-regulating body concerned with letting

Association of Residential Managing Agents *noun* a UK organisation that focuses on the block management of residential property

assumable mortgage *noun US* a mortgage that can be passed to another person

assurance *noun* insurance against something that is certain to happen, e.g. death, rather than against something that might happen, e.g. damage to property

assure *verb* to insure someone against something that is certain to happen, rather than against something that might happen

assured periodic tenancy *noun* a tenancy that gives a legal right to live in a property on a week-to-week or month-to-month basis

assured shorthold agreement *noun* a tenancy that gives the landlord the right to repossess the property at the end of an agreed period of tenancy that may be of any length, not necessarily 'short'

assured shorthold tenancy *noun* a tenancy allowing a landlord to bypass the usual grounds for regaining possession of an assured tenancy (NOTE: The Housing Act 1996 states that, from the 28th February 1997, a landlord will no longer be required to give notice to the tenant and as of this date all new tenancies will automatically be classified as assured shorthold tenancies unless otherwise specified in the contract.)

assured tenancy *noun* (*in England and Wales*) a lease that gives a tenant limited security of tenure and allows a landlord a specific means of terminating a lease

assurer *noun* a company that provides assurance

ASU insurance *abbreviation* accident, sickness and unemployment insurance

atria *noun* plural of **atrium**

atrium *noun* a central hall, usually with a glass roof or skylight and extending the full height or several storeys of a building

auction *noun* a sale of goods or property at which intending buyers bid against one another for individual items, each of which is sold to the bidder offering the highest price (NOTE: When a property is sold at auction, 10% of its value is payable on the day of the sale and the remaining balance within 28 days. Over 300,000 homes are sold at auction in the UK each year.)

auctioneer *noun* the person who conducts an auction

Australian mortgage *noun* a mortgage that offers flexibility in relation to payments, e.g. allowing for extra payments to be made or payment holidays to be taken

Austrian blind *noun* a window blind consisting of a curtain which is raised using a cord

autobolt *noun* a bolt that is operated by a spring mechanism to lock a door automatically when it is closed

Automated Clearing House *noun* a US organisation set up by the federal authorities to settle transactions carried out by computer, e.g. automatic mortgage payments and trade payments between businesses. Abbreviation **ACH**

a vendre *noun* (*in France*) for sale

average house price *noun* the average cost of a house in a particular area of the country (NOTE: See Supplement for 2006 data on average house prices in the UK)

ayuntamiento *noun* (*in Spain*) a local town hall

B

back door *noun* a door or entrance at the rear of a building

back yard *noun* a yard behind a house

bailiff *noun* in the UK excluding Scotland, a legal officer who serves under a sheriff and is empowered to take possession of a debtor's property, forcibly if necessary, to serve writs and to make arrests (NOTE: In Scotland, these duties are undertaken by a *sheriff officer*.)

balance *noun* a remaining or outstanding amount, e.g. the amount of a mortgage that remains to be paid

balcony *noun* a platform projecting from the interior or exterior wall of a building, usually enclosed by a rail or parapet

ballast *noun* **1.** stones or gravel when used as a foundation for a road or railway track **2.** gravel used in making concrete and in earthworks

ballcock *noun* a mechanism that closes the valve in a cistern, in the form of a lever with a floating hollow ball at the end

baluster *noun* an upright post supporting a handrail, e.g. in the banister of a staircase

banister *noun* a handrail supported by posts running up the outside edge of a staircase

bank *noun* a business that keeps money for individual people or companies, exchanges currencies, makes loans and offers other financial services

banker's draft *noun* a bill of exchange drawn by one bank on another, which constitutes cleared funds

Bank of England *noun* the UK central bank, owned by the state, which, together with the Treasury, regulates the nation's finances (NOTE: The Bank of England is responsible for setting the base rate of interest each year.)

bankrupt *adjective* declared by a court to be not capable of paying debts ∎ *noun* someone who has been declared by a court to be not capable of paying debts and whose affairs have been put into the hands of a trustee ∎ *verb* to make someone become bankrupt

bankruptcy *noun* the state of having been legally declared bankrupt

Bankruptcy Court *noun* a court that deals with bankruptcies

barge board *noun* a wooden or uPVC strip that forms the vertical surface of a gable, covering the ends of the rafters

barrister *noun* (*in England and Wales*) a lawyer who can plead or argue a case in one of the higher courts

base *noun* the lower part of a built structure such as a wall, pillar or column

baseboard *noun US* same as **skirting board**

base coat *noun* a thin layer of something such as paint or plaster. used to make a surface smooth and even before applying the top coat.

base course *noun* the bottom layer of an asphalt pavement

basement *noun* **1.** a storey of a building that is wholly or partly below ground level **2.** the foundation, substructure or lowest part of a wall or building

basement flat *noun* a flat in the basement of a building

baseplate *noun* a plate at the foot of a steel column or post, by which it is fixed in place

base rate *noun* a rate of interest set by the Bank of England, used by financial institutions as a basis for setting their various interest rates

base rate tracker mortgage *noun* a mortgage with an interest rate that varies according to changes in the Bank of England's base rate

basic annual income *noun* a person's gross annual income, not including bonuses and other benefits, used by financial institutions as a basis for calculating the amount of money that may be borrowed as a mortgage

basic sum assured *noun* the amount of a mortgage loan that an insurance company guarantees to repay under the terms of an endowment policy

basin *noun* an open metal, ceramic, or plastic container with sloping sides, typically used for holding water or washing

bastion *noun* a projecting part of a wall, rampart or other fortification

bath panel *noun* a panel fitted to the side of a bath to mask the shape of the bath and give a flush square appearance

bathroom *noun* **1.** a room containing a bath or shower and, usually, a washbasin and a toilet **2.** a room with a toilet

bathroom fittings *plural noun* items such as medicine cabinets, towel rails and toilet holders

batten *noun* **1.** a thin strip of wood used in building, e.g. to seal or reinforce a joint or to support laths, slates or tiles **2.** a long narrow piece of wood used for flooring

battening *noun* narrow strips of wood used for covering joints between panels or boards

bay *noun* **1.** a section of a wall or building between two vertical structures such as pillars or buttresses **2.** a recess or alcove in a wall **3.** same as **bay window**

bay window *noun* a window that projects outwards, creating a recess indoors. Also called **bay 3**

BBA *abbreviation* British Bankers' Association

bead *noun* an edge or rim that sticks out on a building or a piece of furniture, traditionally with a pattern of rounded knobs

bead of mastic *noun* a line of mastic applied to a surface

beam *noun* a horizontal structure that spans a gap and supports a floor, roof or other structure above it

bearing load *noun* the amount of weight that a load-bearing wall supports or can support

bearing partition *noun* an interior partition wall that supports some weight, e.g. ceiling joists or bathroom fixtures

bearing point *noun* the point at which a load such as a ceiling joist bears down on a load-bearing wall

bearing wall *noun* same as **load-bearing wall**

bearing weight *noun* same as **bearing load**

bed and breakfast *noun* a small hotel or, more often, a private home that offers overnight accommodation and breakfast for paying guests

bedding *noun* **1.** the mattress, pillows and coverings such as sheets, quilts and blankets used for preparing a bed **2.** a layer of material put down under something else, especially to serve as a foundation

bedrock *noun* the solid rock beneath a layer of soil, rock fragments or gravel

bedroom *noun* a room that has a bed in it and is used mainly for sleeping

bedroom-rated policy *noun* a type of home insurance policy in which the premium is calculated according to the number of bedrooms in the house

before tax income *noun* same as **gross income**

Belfast sink *noun* a traditional ceramic sink basin with a thick wall

benching *noun* the layer of concrete in a manhole between the channels and the brickwork

benefactor *noun* someone who gives property or money to others, especially in a will

beneficial interest *noun* the right of the beneficiary of a property to occupy it or receive rent from it while it is owned by a trustee

beneficial occupier *noun* someone who occupies a property but does not own it

beneficial owner *noun* the true or ultimate owner whose interest may be concealed by a nominee

beneficial use *noun* the right to use, occupy or receive rent from a property that is owned by a trustee

beneficiary *noun* **1.** someone who is left property in a will **2.** someone whose property is administered by a trustee

bevelled edge *noun* a sloping or rounded edge, e.g. on a flooring board

bidet *noun* a low bathroom plumbing fixture resembling a toilet and equipped with a spray or jet of water, used for washing the genital and anal areas

bid price *noun* (*in Scotland*) a price that someone offers to pay for a property

bifold door *noun* a door that folds in the middle, used for cupboards and wardrobes

bilan de santé *noun* (*in France*) a type of survey broadly equivalent to a full structural survey

bill of exchange *noun* a document setting out an instruction to pay a particular person a fixed sum of money on a particular date or when the person requests payment

bill of sale *noun* **1.** a document that the seller gives to the buyer to show that the sale has taken place **2.** a document given to a lender by a borrower to show that the lender owns the property as security for the loan

bipass door *noun* a door that slides behind another door, used for cupboards and wardrobes

bitumen *noun* a sticky mixture of hydrocarbons found in substances such as asphalt and tar

bitumen emulsion *noun* a mixture of bitumen and water, with emulsifying and stabilising agents added, used in making road surfaces

bleed *verb* to allow unwanted air to escape from a radiator by opening a valve at the top

bleed key *noun* a device that opens a bleed valve at the top of a radiator to allow unwanted air to escape

blind *noun* a device that is pulled down to shut out the light from a window, available in various styles

blind bid *noun* (*in Scotland*) an offer on a house made in competition with other offers and with no knowledge of the competing amounts offered

block construction *noun* any system in which surfaces are created by fitting together blocks of a substance, e.g. concrete blocks or aerated blocks

block paving *noun* paving that consists of brick-like blocks arranged in any of various patterns

blockwork *noun* the block structure of something such as a wall

blueprint *noun* a photographic print of a technical drawing with white lines printed on a blue background, or a similarly produced print with blue lines on a white background, usually used as a reference before and during the building process of an architectural or engineering design

bluestone *noun* a blue-grey variety of sandstone used for building and paving

board *noun* **1.** a piece of wood cut into a flat rectangular shape, especially a long narrow piece used for building **2.** a rigid sheet material such as plywood made by compressing layers of other materials

Board of Inland Revenue *noun* the ruling body of the Inland Revenue, appointed by the Treasury

boat level *noun* a small spirit level

boiler *noun* a large tank in which water is heated and stored, either as hot water or as steam, and used for heating a property

boiler efficiency database *noun* a UK database holding information on current and obsolete boilers for the purpose of carrying out energy ratings

bolster *noun* **1.** a long firm cylindrical pillow placed under other pillows to support them **2.** a short horizontal timber positioned between the top of a post and the beam it supports, to spread the load of the post

bona vacantia *noun* a piece of property that has no owner, or no obvious owner, and usually passes to the Crown, as it does in the case of the estate of a person without living relatives dying without having made a will

bond *verb* **1.** to stick together, or make two surfaces stick together **2.** to lay bricks or tiles so that they overlap in a pattern ■ *noun* any of the various combinations of courses in which bricks are laid for strength and decorative effect

Borough Council *noun* the local authority of a town or a district of a large city in England and Wales

borough planner *noun* same as **town planner**

borrower *noun* someone who borrows money, e.g. in the form of a mortgage

borrowing power *noun* the amount of money that a company or individual can borrow

borse immobiliari *noun* (*in Italy*) a centralised property database that contains listings of properties up for sale with accredited estate agents

boundary *noun* the official line that divides one area of land from another

boundary agreement *noun* an agreement between the owners of adjacent properties as to which areas belong to each owner, reached either for the purpose of identifying boundaries or, effectively, for the purpose of transferring ownership of parts of land

box room *noun* a small room in a house, usually too small to be used as a bedroom

brace *noun* **1.** a device that keeps something steady or holds two things together **2.** a device of varying design and positioning used for holding a structural member in place ■ *verb* to support or strengthen something, especially part of a building, with a clamping device

brazing rod *noun* a tool that produces a very hot flame, used for joining pieces of metal using the brazing method, in which a molten copper-zinc alloy is used to seal the metal parts

breach of contract, breach of covenant *noun* an act of breaking a written legal contract (NOTE: If there is a breach of contract during a property transaction, the person affected may have recourse to legal action and/or ask for the contract to be dissolved.)

breach of covenant *noun US* same as **breach of contract**

breach of trust *noun* a failure on the part of a trustee to act properly in regard to a trust

break clause *noun* a right to terminate a lease at one or more specified dates

breaker *noun* same as **circuit breaker**

breaking hammer *noun* a tool that looks like a pneumatic drill and is used like one but is powered by electricity

break the chain *verb* to decide not to proceed with a purchase or sale of property and therefore affect or jeopardise other purchases and sales that depend on it

brick *noun* **1.** a rectangular block of clay or a similar material that is baked until it is hard and is used for building houses, walls and other large permanent structures (NOTE: The most common types of brick are wirecut, in which a column of extruded clay is cut into blocks by wire, stock bricks, made using a mechanised moulding process, and handmade bricks, made individually by hand in a mould.) **2.** bricks collectively, or the material they are made of ■ *verb* **1.** to use bricks to build something or as a liner or paving material **2.** to close something up or wall something off with bricks and mortar

brick and block construction *noun* a method of building that features an internal skin made of concrete blocks or breeze blocks, as distinct from a timber frame, and an external skin of brick

brick guard *noun* a safety mesh attached to scaffolding to prevent materials falling through handrails

brick ledge *noun* the part of a foundation on which the outer brick skin of a timber-frame house will rest

bricks-and-mortar *adjective* used for describing the fixed assets of a company, especially its buildings

brick tie *noun* any of various metal fixings for brick, especially a fixing used between skins of brick to reinforce them

brickwork *noun* **1.** the brick structure of something such as a wall **2.** the technique or skill of laying bricks

bridging loan *noun* a short-term loan given to help someone buy a new house when the old one has not yet been sold

bridleway *noun* a right of way on which members of the public may travel on foot, on bicycles or on horseback

brine extraction search *noun* a check, conducted on behalf of a prospective housebuyer, for evidence of salt-mining in the area of the house, which may lead to concerns over subsidence

British Approval Board of Telecommunications *noun* a UK organisation that certifies products and services in the fields of IT, radio and telecommunications

British Association of Removers *noun* the largest UK trade association for the removals industry

British Bankers' Association *noun* an organisation representing British banks. Abbreviation **BBA**

British Property Federation *noun* a UK trade association that represents the interests of the property-owning and investing industry

British Standards Institute *noun* the national standards organisation for the UK that certifies that products and services meet particular standards. Abbreviation **BSI**

British subsidiary *noun* a British-based company owned by another, usually larger overseas company

British Wood Preserving and Damp Proofing Association *noun* a UK trade association for the timber-preservation and building-preservation industries

broiler *noun US* a grill on a cooker

broker fee *noun* a fee paid to a mortgage broker

brownfield land *noun* land that was previously used for industrial sites and where new buildings can now be constructed

brown goods *plural noun* electrical household entertainment appliances such as televisions, music systems and personal computers

BSI *abbreviation* British Standards Institute

budget *noun* a plan specifying how resources, especially time or money, will be allocated or spent during a particular period or on a particular project ■ *verb* to plan the allocation, expenditure or use of resources, especially money or time

budget planner *noun* a system or piece of software that allows companies and individuals to monitor expenditure and income and plan the finance for future projects

buffer zone *noun* an area designed to form a barrier that prevents potential conflict or harmful contact

build *verb* **1.** to make a structure by fitting the parts of it together **2.** to have a building or other structure made

builder *noun* a person or company engaged in building or repairing houses or other large structures

builders' merchant *noun* a company that sells tools and materials to the building trade

Builders' Merchants Federation *noun* a UK trade organisation for builders, plumbers, heating engineers and timber merchants

builder's risk insurance *noun* insurance that covers a building contractor for a broad scope of eventualities related to various aspects of construction

building *noun* a structure with walls and a roof, e.g. a house or factory

Building Act *noun* a piece of UK legislation in which regulations are made about the design and construction of buildings and the provision of services in connection with buildings

building block *noun* a large block of concrete or similar hard material, used for building houses and other large structures

building contractor *noun* a company or person with a formal contract to do a construction job, supplying labour and materials and providing and overseeing staff if needed

building control *noun* a system for regulating the design of buildings, especially for the safety and health of the occupants

building control certificate *noun* a certificate, issued by a local authority building control department, stating that building work has been carried out in accordance with minimum standards stipulated in building regulations

building control consent *noun* official permission from a local authority to proceed with a proposed building project

building control officer *noun* a local authority official responsible for ensuring that proposed building projects comply with building regulations

Building Cost Information Service *noun* an information service provided by the Royal Institution of Chartered Surveyors

Building LifePlans scheme *noun* a UK scheme under which assessments of the durability of new buildings are carried out

building management system *noun* a computer system that automates the various mechanical and electrical systems, e.g. heating and lighting, that operate in a large building

building notice *noun* a notice of the intention to construct a building that forms part of an application for planning permission

building permit *noun* an official document that allows someone to build on a piece of land

building plot *noun* a site on which new building is proposed

building preservation *noun* the practice of making sure that old buildings are kept in good condition

building preservation notice *noun* a notice that is served to protect a building under imminent threat of demolition or alteration

building products index *noun* an index of UK manufacturers and suppliers of building products

building regulations *noun* national regulations on the precise method of constructing a new building, set out in the Building Regulations Act 1991 and enforced by local authority building control officials (NOTE: Current UK building regulations cover structural issues, insulation, use of toxic substances, hygiene measures, ventilation, drainage, fuel storage, fire safety and disabled access.)

Building Research Establishment *noun* a UK company that offers a range of consultancy, testing and research services covering all aspects of the built environment

buildings insurance *noun* insurance cover that protects against damage to the fabric of a building, as distinct from its contents

building standards indemnity scheme *noun* any scheme offering protection against defects in newbuild properties, e.g. the NHBC Buildmark scheme

building survey *noun* a comprehensive and relatively costly type of survey carried out on behalf of the prospective buyer of a property

building warrant *noun* (*in Scotland*) a document giving official permission from a local authority to proceed with a proposed building project or with an alteration to an existing building

Buildmark scheme *noun* a structural guarantee that covers the purchaser of a new house against any physical damage to the home caused by a defect that results from the builder failing to construct in accordance with NHBC standards

built environment *noun* the part of our surroundings which consists of man-made structures such as buildings and roads

built-in appliance *noun* an appliance such as a cooker or dishwasher that is a part of a room that cannot be removed

built-up *adjective* containing many buildings

bulb *noun* same as **lightbulb**

bulb holder *noun* a light fixture into which a lightbulb fits directly

bulky item *noun* a large waste item that is not normally collected as part of a domestic refuse collection service

bulky item collection *noun* a special refuse collection service for bulky items

bulldoze *verb* to demolish a building or clear debris using a bulldozer

bund *noun* a soil wall built across a slope to retain water or to hold waste in a sloping landfill site

bungalow *noun* a single-storey house

burden *noun* (*in Scotland*) an encumbrance or other limitation affecting the ownership or use of property

burdens section *noun* (*in Scotland*) the sections of the title deeds or land certificate in which details of the relevant burdens can be found

business day *noun* any day except Saturdays, Sundays or bank holidays

business lease *noun* an agreement to rent a business property for a specified period of time

business premises *plural noun* a building or set of buildings and land used for the purpose of carrying out a business activity

business purposes *plural noun* the purposes of carrying on a commercial activity of some kind

business rates *plural noun* a payment made to a local authority by the owner or occupier of business premises as a contribution to the cost of local services (NOTE: Some types of business and organisation are exempt form paying business rates, for example agricultural and sewage business, places of worship and some properties for use by disabled people.)

business tenancy *noun* the tenancy of an individual or company renting a property for business purposes

buttress *noun* a solid structure, usually made of brick or stone, that is built against a wall to support it ■ *verb* to support a wall with a buttress

buyer *noun* someone who buys or intends to buy something

buyer beware *noun* the notion that a buyer is responsible for ensuring that the item about to be purchased is fit for its intended purpose

buyer's market *noun* a market where products are sold cheaply because there are few people who want to buy them. Opposite **seller's market**

buying agent *noun* a person who buys for a business or another person and earns a commission

buy to let mortgage *noun* a mortgage offered to someone buying a property in order to let it as an investment, rather than occupy it as a home

byway *noun* a small side road not regularly used by people or traffic

C

cable *verb* to connect a building or area to a cable telecommunications network

cable and tracer detector *noun* full form of **CAT detector**

cable detector *noun* a device for locating underground cables, e.g. in order to carry out repairs or in order to avoid them during building work

CAD *abbreviation* computer aided design

cadastre *noun* (*in France*) a local planning office

caderneta urbana *noun* (*in Portugal*) a document issued by the tax office that outlines such details as the size of a property, its borders and its rateable value

CAD technician *noun* someone who can produce plans or architectural drawings using the techniques of computer aided design

caisson *noun* same as **coffer**

Campaign for the Abolition of Residential Leaseholds *noun* a lobby group that campaigns for the abolition of the leasehold system of land ownership, a system under which almost all flats and many houses are owned in England and Wales

candela *noun* an SI unit measuring the brightness of a light. Symbol **cd**

canopy *noun* **1.** a covering fixed above something to provide shelter or for decoration, especially a fabric covering that can be removed or folded away **2.** a roofed structure that covers an area, especially one that shelters a passageway between two buildings

cantilever *noun* a bracket that supports a balcony or a cornice

cap and collar mortgage *noun* a mortgage guaranteeing that the interest rate charged will remain between two specified levels

caparra confirmatoria *noun* (*in Italy*) a deposit paid on the purchase of a property, forfeited if the prospective buyer pulls out

caparra penitenziale *noun* (*in Italy*) a deposit paid on the purchase of a property that gives neither the purchaser nor the vendor the right to take the other party to court to force the deal

capital *noun* **1.** the money, property and assets used in a business **2.** a town or city where the government of a province or country is situated

capital allowance *noun* a variable tax reduction resulting from expenditure on items such as plant and machinery used in connection with the business

capital and interest mortgage *noun* a mortgage in which the payments made reduce both the interest payable and the amount of the initial loan

capital assets *plural noun* property or machinery that a company owns and uses in its business

capital gain *noun* an amount of money made by selling a fixed asset. Opposite **capital loss**

capital gains tax *noun* the tax payable where an asset has increased in value during the period of ownership. Abbreviation **CGT** (NOTE: CGT is usually not payable on the sale of a property which has been used as the seller's main home, provided certain conditions are met. See www.direct.gov.uk for more details.)

capital raising *noun* the process of arranging finance to buy property

capital reducing mortgage *noun* same as **capital and interest mortgage**

capped rate *noun* a rate of interest that will not exceed a specified limit

capped rate mortgage *noun* a mortgage that offers a rate of interest that will not exceed a specified limit

capstone *noun* a stone used at the top of a wall or another structure

care and repair scheme *noun* a scheme designed to enable old and disabled owner-occupiers to remain living in their own homes by providing assistance with housing repairs, improvements or adaptations

carpentry *noun* **1.** the work or occupation of building and repairing things made of wood such as houses and boats, or the wooden parts of them **2.** the work or objects produced by a carpenter

carpet *noun* a piece of thick heavy fabric covering the floor of a room or area ■ *verb* to cover a floor, or the floor of a room, with a carpet

carte professionnelle *noun* (*in France*) an estate agent's licence to practise

case management *noun* the process of managing the property dealings of solicitors and estate agents, or a piece of software designed to facilitate this

casement stay *noun* a bar that keeps a casement window in an open position

casement window *noun* a window that is hinged at the side to open out or in, as distinct, e.g., from a sash window that slides to open

cashback *noun* an amount of money that is offered as an incentive to buy something, e.g. to buy one of the mortgage products of a particular lender

cash buyer *noun* a buyer of property who can buy outright, without the need for a mortgage

cash incentive scheme *noun* a grant from a local authority to help someone buy a private house and relinquish a council tenancy, repayable in part or in whole

cash in value *noun* the value of an insurance policy at a particular time before maturity

casing *noun* **1.** an outer covering, e.g. the sheath of an electrical cable **2.** a frame containing a door, window or stairway

castor *noun* a small wheel on a mount that allows it to turn in all directions, attached under the corners of heavy furniture and other objects to make them easier to move

castor cup *noun* a disc placed under a castor on furniture to protect a floor or carpet

casualty insurance *noun* a broad category of insurance that includes almost all areas not related to life, health or property

CAT detector *noun* a device used for detecting unseen items such as underground water pipes or concealed cables. Full form **cable and tracer detector**

CAT mark *noun* a logo indicating that a financial product meets certain standards on charges, access and terms

CAT mortgage *noun* a mortgage that meets certain standards on charges, access and terms

CAT standard *noun* a set of standards for financial products, abandoned by the UK government in 2005

caulking *noun* a flexible sealant substance similar to mastic

caveat *noun* something said as a warning, caution or qualification

caveat emptor *noun* the principle in a property transaction that the buyer should look carefully for flaws in the property, as the seller cannot be held responsible for them after completion (NOTE: **Caveat emptor** is a Latin phrase and is usually translated as 'let the buyer beware'.)

cavity membrane *noun* any of various substances built into cavity walls to provide heat insulation or damp proofing

cavity wall *noun* an external wall of a building that is made up of two leaves of masonry, bricks, or blocks separated by a cavity (NOTE: This prevents moisture penetration and improves thermal insulation.)

cavity wall insulation *noun* any of various types of insulating substance inserted or built into cavity walls to enhance a building's heat retention

cavity wall tie *noun* a metal tie fitted across a cavity wall between skins of blocks or bricks as a structural reinforcement

CCJ *abbreviation* county court judgment

CCTV drain inspection *noun* the use of a closed-circuit television system to inspect areas of drains to which human access is impossible

cédula de habitabilidad *noun* (*in Spain*) a document issued by the local town hall certifying that a property is fit for habitation

ceiling *noun* the overhead surface of a room

ceiling hanger *noun* a bracket to which panels are fitted to form a suspended ceiling

ceiling joist *noun* a joist to which boards are fitted to form a ceiling

ceiling price *noun* the highest price that can be reached

ceiling tile *noun* a tile of varying material fitted to a ceiling to form a decorative surface

cellar *noun* a room wholly or partly underground that is used for storage, traditionally for the storage of wine or food

cement *noun* **1.** a fine grey powder of limestone and clay, mixed with water and sand to make mortar, or with water, sand and aggregate to make concrete **2.** a building material that sets hard to form concrete, made by mixing cement with water, sand and aggregate **3.** a glue or similar bonding substance

cement mixer *noun* **1.** a transportable machine with a revolving drum in which cement powder, water, sand and other materials can be mixed to make concrete, mortar or stucco. Also called **concrete mixer 2.** a truck with a large revolving drum for mixing, transporting and pouring concrete

central heating *noun* a system designed to heat a whole building from a single source of heat by pumping hot water or air to room radiators or vents

central heating cooker *noun* a type of cooker that also functions as a boiler for a central heating system

central vacuum system *noun* a system of wall vents around a property that use suction to remove dust and debris brushed into them, or into which lightweight appliances may be connected for easy vacuuming

Centre for Non Residents *noun* a division of HM Revenue and Customs dedicated to people who are not resident in the UK but who pay National Insurance and other contributions or who receive income from a UK source

certidão do registo predial *noun* (*in Portugal*) the title deeds to a property

certificado de fin de obra *noun* (*in Spain*) a certificate confirming the completion of a building

certificat d'urbanisme *noun* (*in France*) a certificate that outlines the planning status of a particular property

certificate of completion *noun* a certificate submitted to a local authority to indicate that proposed building work has been completed

certificate of title *noun* a record of the ownership of property

certificate of value *noun* a certificate, provided by a surveyor, stating a reasonable estimate of the value of a property

certificato di abitabilitá *noun* (*in Italy*) a certificate that confirms that a property is fit for human habitation

certified copy *noun* a document that is certified as being exactly the same in content as the original

cession *noun* the act of giving up property to someone, especially a creditor

cesspit *noun* a pit for the collection of waste matter and water, especially sewage

cesspool *noun* a covered underground tank or well for the collection of waste matter and water, especially sewage

CGT *abbreviation* capital gains tax

chain *noun* **1.** a number of potential buyers and sellers of property each of whose separate property transactions depends to an extent on the transactions of the others, with the result that others are jeopardised if one falls through **2.** in construction, an accessory used for lifting heavy items

chain-free *adjective* used for describing a property transaction that does not depend on the transactions of others (NOTE: A chain-free transaction is extremely desirable, as it is not subject to last-minute problems caused by other transactions in the chain being delayed or falling through.)

chalet *noun* a house or cottage traditionally made of wood with wide overhanging eaves, in a style originally built in Switzerland

chalk soil, chalky soil *noun* very hard soil that contains a high proportion of calcium carbonate

chamber *noun* **1.** a reception room in an official residence or palace **2.** a room used for a particular purpose

Chambre des Experts Immobiliers *noun* (*in France*) the regulatory body for French surveyors

chancel repairs search *noun* a search that reveals whether the owner of a property will be liable to contribute towards repairs to the local parish church

change of use *noun* an official notice allowing a property to be used in a different way, e.g. a house to be used as a business office, or a shop to be used as a factory

CHAPS *noun* an electronic, bank-to-bank payment system that guarantees same-day payment. Full form **clearing house automated payment system**

CHAPS fee *noun* a fee that businesses pay to use the CHAPS payment system

character *noun* qualities that make a property interesting or attractive

character referee *noun* someone who provides a statement vouching for the good character of a potential tenant

charge *noun* a creditor's legal right to receive money from the sale or lease of the property of a debtor

chargeable *adjective* **1.** liable or able to be charged to a person, organisation or account **2.** used for describing property or land capable of being subject to a charge

charge certificate *noun* a certificate that proves or officially transfers ownership of property

chargee *noun* someone who holds a charge over a property

charges register *noun* a register of information relating to properties in a particular area, giving details such as whether a property is subject to a smoke-control order

charging order *noun* a court order made in favour of a creditor, granting him or her a charge over a debtor's property

Chartered Institute of Arbitrators *noun* a UK organisation that provides training and qualifications in arbitration, mediation and adjudication

Chartered Institute of Architectural Technologists *noun* a UK body representing professionals who provide architectural design services and solutions and who are specialists in the science of architecture, building design and construction

Chartered Institute of Building *noun* a UK body representing professionals involved in the management of the total building process

Chartered Institute of Housing *noun* a UK professional body representing people who work in all areas of housing

chase *noun* a channel, groove or trench for something such as a pipe to lie in or fit into ■ *verb* to cut or grind a channel, groove or trench in something

chattel mortgage *noun US* a mortgage in which personal property is used as security

chattels personal *noun* any property which is moveable

chattels real *noun* leaseholds

chimney *noun* **1.** a hollow vertical structure, usually made of brick or steel, that allows gas, smoke or steam from a fire or furnace to escape into the atmosphere **2.** the part of a chimney that rises above the roof of a building. Also called **chimney stack 3.** a passage or pipe inside a chimney through which smoke or steam escapes

chimney stack *noun* same as **chimney 2**

chinagraph pencil *noun* a drawing instrument for use on acetate, glass and other impermeable surfaces

Chinese bond *noun* a style of bricklaying in which bricks are laid on their edges, producing cavities between the leaves of brick

chipboard *noun* a construction material made from compressed wood chips held together by a synthetic resin and produced in the form of hard flat boards

chisel *noun* a tool for cutting and shaping wood or stone, consisting of a straight flat bevelled blade with a sharp square-cut bottom edge inserted in a handle, worked with the hand or held in one hand and struck with a hammer or mallet ■ *verb* to carve, cut or work wood or stone using a chisel

chromated copper arsenate *noun* a substance used as a wood preservative

Chubb lock *noun* any of a range of locks manufacture by the Chubb company, regarded as very safe

cill *noun* same as **sill**

circuit breaker *noun* an electrical device used to interrupt an electrical supply when there is too much current flow

cistern *noun* **1.** a tank for storing water, especially one in the roof of a house or connected to a toilet **2.** an underground tank for storing rainwater

Citizens' Advice Bureaux *plural noun* a network of local offices established to help people resolve their legal, money and other problems by providing free information and advice

civic amenity site *noun* a local-authority facility for the disposal of refuse, usually consisting of a landfill site and recycling points

civil action *noun* a court case brought by a person or a company against someone who is alleged to have done them wrong

civil court *noun* a court where civil actions are heard

civil engineer *noun* a person who specialises in the construction of such large infrastructure items as roads, bridges and railways

civil engineering *noun* the construction of such large infrastructure items as roads, bridges and railways

cladding *noun* a layer of stone, tiles or wood added to the outside of a building to protect it against the weather or to improve its insulation or appearance

claim *noun* **1.** an assertion of a legal right **2.** a document used in a county court to start a legal action **3.** a statement that someone has a right to property held by another person **4.** a request for money that you believe you should have ■ *verb* **1.** to state a grievance in court **2.** to ask for money **3.** to say that you have a right to property held by someone else

claim adjustor *noun* same as **loss adjustor**

claimant *noun* **1.** someone who claims something such as state benefits or an inheritance **2.** someone who brings a lawsuit in a civil court against a person or organisation

claim form *noun* **1.** a form that has to be completed when making an insurance claim **2.** a form issued by a court when requested by a claimant, containing the particulars of claim and a statement of value (NOTE: Since the introduction of the new Civil Procedure Rules in April 1999, this term has replaced the **writ of summons**.)

clamp *noun* a mechanical device with movable jaws, used for holding two things firmly together or one object firmly in position ■ *verb* to fasten two or more things firmly together using a clamp

clapboard *noun* a long narrow wooden board that has one edge thicker than the other, used to clad buildings

clause *noun* a distinct section of a document, especially a legal document, that is usually separately numbered

clay mining search *noun* a check, conducted on behalf of a prospective housebuyer, for evidence of clay mining in the area of the house, which may lead to concerns over subsidence

clay soil *noun* heavy wet soil that contains a high proportion of clay

cleared funds *noun* a payment made to a person or company in a form such as cash or a banker's draft, which does not need to be transferred from one bank account to another taking several working days (NOTE: Cleared funds are sometimes requested in property transactions, e.g. when paying a deposit for a rented house.)

clearing house automated payment system *noun* full form of **CHAPS**

clear title *noun* title to property without any charges or other encumbrances

clincher *noun* 1. a nail or rivet that has its protruding end bent over 2. a tool for bending the ends of nails or rivets

cloakroom *noun* a walk-in cupboard in a house, where coats and other outdoor items are stored

close *noun* a residential road, often a cul-de-sac on a modern housing estate

closing date *noun* (*in Scotland*) the deadline by which offers to purchase a property must be received by the selling agent

coal mining search *noun* a check, conducted on behalf of a prospective housebuyer, for evidence of coal mining in the area of the house, which may lead to concerns over subsidence

co-buyer *noun* a person who buys a property jointly with another who may be a friend, a member of the family or a stranger

code of conduct *noun* a set of rules of behaviour by which a group of people work

code of practice *noun* 1. a set of rules to be followed when applying a law 2. a set of rules drawn up by a trade association, which its members must adhere to in their work

codice fiscale *noun* (*in Italy*) a tax number, similar to a national insurance number, that is needed in order to complete a property transaction

coffer *noun* 1. an ornamental sunken panel in a ceiling or dome. Also called **caisson** 2. same as **cofferdam**

cofferdam *noun* a temporary watertight structure that is pumped dry to enclose an area underwater and allow construction work on a ship, bridge or rig to be carried out

cohabit *verb* to live together, especially without being formally married

cohabitant *noun* same as **cohabitee**

cohabitation *noun* the practice of living together as husband and wife, whether legally married or not

cohabitation agreement *noun* a written agreement that sets out the conditions under which two people live together as if in marriage, and sets out their financial obligations towards each other

cohabitee, cohabiter *noun* a person with whom another lives as if in marriage. Also called **cohabitant**

coir *noun* a coarse natural fibre that comes from the husk of the coconut, used for making matting

collared rate mortgage *noun* a mortgage in which the interest rate will not fall below a certain level for a specified period

collateral *noun* property or goods used as security against a loan and forfeited if the loan is not repaid

collective investment fund *noun* a fund that allows several individuals to invest money together, enabling them to participate in a wider range of investments or properties than may be feasible for an individual investor

column *noun* an upright support shaped like a long cylinder

combination boiler *noun* a boiler that heats water for a central heating system and delivers hot water directly to taps, without the need for a hot-water cylinder

combustible *adjective* able or likely to catch fire and burn

combustion appliance *noun* any appliance that burns fuel for heating, cooking or decorative purposes

commercial conveyancing *noun* conveyancing that relates to commercial property

commercial improvement area *noun* an area earmarked by a local authority for commercial redevelopment, within which grants are available for commercial projects

commercial property standard enquiries *noun* a set of proposed industry-standard pre-contract enquiries to be raised in transactions involving commercial property subject to tenancies, drafted by the London Property Support Lawyers Group

commission *noun* a fee paid to an agent for providing a service, especially a percentage of the total amount of business transacted (NOTE: See note at **estate agency fees**.)

Commissioners of Inland Revenue *noun* same as **Board of Inland Revenue**

Commission for Architecture and the Built Environment *noun* a UK government commission advising on architecture, urban design and public space, working directly with architects, planners, designers, developers and private clients

common *adjective* belonging to or shared by two or more people

common areas *plural noun* areas within or surrounding a block of flats or similar development that are shared by all owners, including, e.g., recreation facilities, outdoor space, parking, landscaping, fences and laundry rooms

commonhold *noun* a new type of freehold ownership for owners of flats in a block, in which all flat owners become members of a company (the commonhold association) that owns the freehold and thus the block

Commonhold and Leasehold Reform Act 2002 *noun* a piece of UK legislation that introduced commonhold

commonhold assessment *noun* the contributions each member of a commonhold makes to the cost of running the commonhold

commonhold association *noun* a company formed of the members of a commonhold

commonhold community statement *noun* a legal document that sets out the terms of a commonhold and the responsibilities of its members

commonhold unit *noun* a property owned under commonhold

commonhold unit holder *noun* a co-owner of a property owned under commonhold

commonhold unit information certificate *noun* a certificate completed by a commonhold association at the request of a unit holder, setting out the debts owed to the association in respect of the unit, the commonhold assessment, the reserve fund and any interest on late payments

common land *noun* an area of land to which the public has access for walking

common law *noun* 1. a law established on the basis of decisions by the courts, rather than by statute 2. a general system of laws that formerly were the only laws existing in England, in some cases now superseded by statute (NOTE: You say **at common law** when referring to something happening according to the principles of common law.)

common-law marriage *noun* a form of marriage that has not strictly existed since the Marriage Act of 1753 but which term is often used for referring to the status of the relationship of people who cohabit

common-law spouse *noun* a spouse in a common-law marriage, or, more commonly now, a cohabitee

common ownership *noun* ownership of a property or of a company by a group of people who each own a part

common parts *plural noun* the common areas of a building containing two or more flats, e.g. the entrance hall and the stairwell. Also called **communal areas**

common parts grant *noun* a grant to improve the common parts of a block of flats

common property *noun* (*in Scotland*) property that belongs to two or more owners

common services *plural noun* services such as drainage and lighting that are used by all the owners of a common property

commons registration search *noun* a check, made on behalf of a prospective buyer of a property, to establish whether a piece of land or property is registered as common in the Official Registers kept by the a county council

communal *adjective* used or owned by all members of a group or community

communal areas *plural noun* same as **common parts**

communauté de biens *noun* (*in France*) common ownership of assets, including property, within a marriage

Communities Scotland *noun* an agency of the Scottish Executive that aims to ensure decent housing and strong communities across Scotland

community property *noun* (*in the US, Canada, France and many other countries*) a situation in which a husband and wife jointly own any property that they acquire during the course of their marriage. Compare **separate property**

community right to buy *noun* (*in Scotland*) a right of a member of a community to buy land within it, introduced by the Land Reform (Scotland) Act 2003

commuter belt *noun* an area around a town from which people commute to it

Companies House *noun* (*in the UK*) an office that keeps details of incorporated companies

company search *noun* a check, carried out on behalf of a prospective buyer of property, to ascertain information about a company involved in the property, e.g. in its management, information that might include its other business interests or its financial standing

compensation *noun* an amount of money given to pay for loss or damage

competent landlord *noun* a landlord with a superior interest in a property, who may or may not be the immediate landlord to whom rent is paid

complainant *noun* someone who makes a complaint or who starts proceedings against someone

complaint *noun* **1.** a statement expressing discontent or unhappiness about a fact or situation **2.** a statement setting out the reasons for a legal action

complaints procedure *noun* an agreed way of presenting complaints formally, e.g. from a tenant to the landlord of a property

completion *noun* **1.** the act of finishing something, e.g. the construction of a property **2.** the last stage in the sale of a property when the solicitors for the two parties meet, when the purchaser pays and the vendor passes the conveyance and the deeds to the purchaser

completion date *noun* the date when the solicitors for the two parties meet, when the purchaser pays and the vendor passes the conveyance and the deeds to the purchaser

completion statement *noun* a statement of account from a solicitor to a client showing all the costs of the sale or purchase of a property

compliance *noun* the fact that someone's work or behaviour complies with instructions, regulations or laws

compliant *adjective* made or done in accordance with instructions, regulations or laws

compound *verb* to calculate or pay interest based on both the principal and the previously accrued interest

compound interest *noun* interest that is added to the capital and then earns interest itself

comprehensive insurance *noun* insurance that covers you against a large number and wide range of possible risks

compressor *noun* a machine that compresses gas so that the power produced when the gas is released can be used to power another machine, e.g. a pneumatic drill

compromesso *noun* (*in Italy*) a contract between purchaser and vendor

compromis de vente *noun* (*in France*) a type of preliminary contract that commits both parties to a property transaction. Also called **promesse synallagmatique de vente**

35

compulsory insurance *noun* a requirement to obtain buildings insurance

compulsory purchase *noun* the buying of a property by the local council or the government even if the owner does not want to sell

compulsory purchase order *noun* an official order from a local authority or from the government ordering an owner to sell his or her property

compulsory registration of land *noun* a requirement that the purchaser of land register details of his or her title and all other rights relating to the land

computer aided design *noun* the use of a computer and sophisticated graphics software to design products, e.g. by an architect. Abbreviation **CAD**

comune *noun* (*in Italy*) a local authority

comunidad de bienes *noun* (*in Spain*) the common ownership of assets, including property, within a marriage

comunidad de propietarios *noun* (*in Spain*) a 'community of owners' of properties in a complex, with obligations as to communal areas

conclusion of missives *noun* (*in Scotland*) the point at which the contract between the seller and buyer becomes binding on the parties

concrete *noun* a mixture of cement, sand, aggregate and water in specific proportions that hardens to a strong stony consistency over varying lengths of time

concrete admixture *noun* a material other than cement, aggregate and water that is added to concrete either before or during its mixing to alter properties such as its workability, curing temperature range, set time or colour

concrete board *noun* a panel made out of concrete and fibreglass, usually used as a tile backing material

concrete mixer *noun* same as **cement mixer**

concretor *noun* a worker on a building site who oversees the use of ready-mixed concrete

condensation *noun* tiny drops of water that form on a cold surface such as a window when warmer air comes into contact with it

condensing boiler *noun* a boiler in which exhaust gases are used to pre-heat the water, providing for greater energy efficiency

condensing unit *noun* a device that cools air for an air-conditioning system

condiciones resolutorias *plural noun* (*in Spain*) an escape clause that may form part of the contrato privado de compraventa

condition *noun* **1.** the particular state of repair of something such as a building **2.** a requirement that must be fulfilled, especially in a legal contract ■ *verb* to state a requirement that must be fulfilled, or to make something dependent on a requirement, especially in a legal contract

conditional contract *noun* a contract to transfer ownership of property that places certain conditions on one or both parties

conditional insurance *noun* the fact that a mortgage lender insists on certain types of insurance being taken out before granting a mortgage

conditional offer *noun* (*in Scotland*) an offer to purchase property, subject to a condition or conditions, e.g., that any survey carried out is satisfactory

conditions of sale *plural noun* a list of the terms such as discounts and credit terms under which a sale takes place

conditions suspensives *plural noun* (*in France*) get-out clauses that can form part of a contract for property purchase or sale

condominium *noun* US a system of ownership in which a person owns an individual apartment in a building, together with a share of the land and common parts such as stairs and roof

conduit *noun* **1.** a pipe or channel that carries liquid to or from a place **2.** a pipe or tube that covers and protects electrical cables

Confederation of Roofing Contractors *noun* a UK organisation that promotes good practice in roofing and seeks to protect homeowners from unscrupulous traders

conflict of interest *noun* a situation where a person or firm may profit personally from decisions taken in an official capacity

Consejo Superior de los Colegios de Arquitectos de España *noun* (*in Spain*) the regulatory body for qualified architects. Abbreviation **CSCAE**

consent order *noun* a court order that someone must not do something without the agreement of another party

conservation area *noun* an area of special environmental or historical importance that is protected by law from changes that have not received official permission

conservation area consent *noun* permission to demolish a building in a conservation area

conservation des hypothèques *noun* (*in France*) the Land and Charges Registry, where title deeds to a property must be registered

conservatory *noun* a room with glass walls and roof where plants are grown or displayed, often built onto the side of a house

Considerate Builders Scheme *noun* a scheme established to improve the image of the UK construction industry and encourage good practice

Consiglio dei Notai *noun* (*in Italy*) the professional body for notaries

constant net payment *noun* a type of capital and interest mortgage in which the monthly repayments remain the same throughout the term

construction *noun* **1.** the building of something, especially a large structure such as a house, road or bridge **2.** a structure that has been built **3.** the way in which something has been built, especially with regard to the type and quality of the structure, materials and workmanship **4.** the building industry regarded as a whole

construction company *noun* a company which specialises in building

construction guarantee *noun* a guarantee of build quality provided by a construction company, e.g. an NHBC buildmark

Construction Industry Council *noun* a representative forum for the professional bodies, research organisations and specialist business associations in the construction industry

construction plant *noun* heavy equipment and vehicles used in the construction industry

constructive trust *noun* a trust that is regarded as existing as a result of a person's behaviour

Consumer Credit Act *noun* a piece of UK legislation that requires most businesses that offer goods or services on credit or lend money to consumers to be licensed by the Office of Fair Trading

containment kerb *noun* a high kerb designed to prevent vehicles from running onto structures such as roundabouts

contaminated land *noun* land that has become contaminated as a result of industrial development

contents insurance *noun* insurance cover that protects against damage to or theft of the contents of a building, as distinct from its fabric

continuity tester *noun* a device that tests the electrical wiring in a property and identifies any short circuits

contract *noun* a legal agreement between two or more parties

contract binding *noun* same as **conclusion of missives**

contract for deed *noun* US a written agreement showing the terms of the sale of a property, where the title is only transferred to the purchaser after he has made a stated number of monthly payments

contractor *noun* **1.** a company or person with a formal contract to do a specific job, supplying labour and materials and providing and overseeing staff if needed **2.** one of the parties to a contract

contract race *noun* a situation in which a seller has received and accepted two or more offers on a property and will sell to the party who is ready to exchange contracts first

Contracts (Rights of Third Parties Act) 1999 *noun* a piece of UK legislation introduced with the purpose of giving the right to a third party to enforce a term of a contract to which that third party is not a party

contractual periodic tenancy *noun* a tenancy that runs for an indefinite term on a periodic basis

contrat de réservation *noun* (*in France*) a type of preliminary contract for the purchase of an unfinished property

contrat multirisque habitation *noun* (*in France*) a type of insurance similar to a UK home insurance policy

contrato privado de compraventa *noun* (*in Spain*) the most common preliminary contract in a property purchase that commits both parties to the transaction

contrato promessa de compra e venda *noun* (*in Portugal*) a promissory contract that is legally binding between purchaser and vendor (NOTE: A deposit is payable by the purchaser and if the contract is breached, the deposit will be forfeited.)

contribuição predial *noun* (*in Portugal*) the payment of property taxes

controlled parking zone *noun* an area in which parking restrictions are in force

controlled waste *noun* any of various types of waste, including domestic refuse, the handling and disposal of which is controlled by legislation

Control of Substances Hazardous to Health *noun* a piece of UK legislation introduced with the object of reducing occupational ill health by setting out a framework for controlling hazardous substances in the workplace. Abbreviation **COSHH**

conventional boiler *noun* a boiler that heats water for a central heating system and sends water for taps to a hot-water cylinder to be stored and heated there

conventional building *noun* the methods and materials of construction used in most buildings, as distinct from sustainable or green building

conversion *noun* **1.** a property that has been converted for a new use **2.** the act of dealing with a person's property in a way that is not consistent with that person's rights over it

conversion flat *noun* a flat created by converting a larger property into smaller units

conveyance *noun* **1.** the act of transferring the ownership of land from one person to another **2.** a legal document that transfers the ownership of land from the seller to the buyer

conveyancer *noun* someone who draws up a conveyance

conveyancing *noun* **1.** the process of drawing up the document that legally transfers a property from a seller to a buyer **2.** law and procedure relating to the purchase and sale of property

conveyancing quote *noun* an estimate of how much a conveyancer will charge for the work that you want them to do

Conveyancing Standing Committee *noun* a UK parliamentary committee established to examine suggestions for the reform of conveyancing practice and law

cooler *noun* a compartment or container in which something is cooled or kept cool

cooling fan *noun* any of various electrical devices designed for cooling the air in a room or building

cooling off period *noun* a period of reflection allowed before making a legally binding commitment, e.g. before formally accepting an insurance policy

cooperative *noun* **1.** a business run by a group of employees who are also the owners and who share the profits **2.** (*in the US*) a type of property ownership in which purchasers own a number of shares in a non-profit making corporation and pay towards a mortgage for the whole building, according to the number of shares owned

co-ownership *noun* **1.** an arrangement in which two or more persons own a property **2.** an arrangement in which partners or employees have shares in a company

co-property *noun* ownership of property by two or more people together

copropriété *noun* (*in France*) a property that is made up of several separate properties, e.g. a block of flats

co-proprietor *noun* someone who owns a property with another person or several other people

corbel *noun* a bracket of brick or stone that juts out of a wall to support a structure above it ■ *verb* **1.** to lay stones or bricks in layers so that each juts out above the one below to form a supporting bracket **2.** to support a cornice or other structure on corbels

CORGI *abbreviation* Council for Registered Gas Installers

corner bead *noun* a metal trim that forms the basis for an outside corner on a plasterboard wall

corner board *noun* any of various strip sections that form the inside or outside corners of a wall, e.g. on a clapboard house

cornerstone *noun* **1.** a stone joining two walls where they meet at a corner **2.** the first stone laid at a corner where two walls begin and form the first part of a new building

corner unit *noun* a piece of furniture of varying shape and function designed to sit in a corner

cornice *noun* **1.** a projecting horizontal moulding along the top of a wall or building **2.** a decorative plaster moulding around a room where the walls and ceiling meet **3.** (*in classical architecture*) the top projecting section of the entablature, the part of a building that is supported by the columns ■ *verb* to decorate or finish a wall or building with a cornice

corporeal hereditaments *plural noun* rights in respect of property that physically exists, e.g. a house or furniture

corridor *noun* a passage between parts of a building, often with a series of rooms opening onto it

co-seller *noun* an individual or company with whom another is selling a property that they jointly own

COSHH *abbreviation* Control of Substances Hazardous to Health

cost of living expenses *plural noun* expenses incurred by someone who is temporarily not living in his or her usual place of residence, e.g. the cost of food or transport

cost of rebuilding *noun* an assessment of the cost of rebuilding a house, which is a feature of buildings insurance

cottage *noun* a small house, usually situated in the countryside

council estate *noun* an area of housing developed and largely managed by a local authority, often with amenities such as shops and community centres

Council for Licensed Conveyancers *noun* the UK regulatory body for specialist property lawyers known as Licensed Conveyancers

Council for Registered Gas Installers *noun* the national UK watchdog for gas safety, with whom registration is now a legal requirement for businesses and self-employed people working on gas fittings or appliances. Abbreviation **CORGI**

council house *noun* a house on a council estate

council housing *noun* houses on a council estate

Council of the Notariats of the European Union *noun* an organisation that represents the notarial profession in European institutions, handling negotiation and decision-making for all civil law notaries in the European Union

council safety inspection *noun* same as **safety inspection**

council tax *noun* a tax paid by individuals or companies to a local authority, introduced in April 1993 as a replacement for the much maligned community charge, or 'poll tax', and calculated in relation to the value of the residential or commercial property occupied

council tax band *noun* a category which determines how much council tax must be paid on a house, based on its value at the time of last valuation (NOTE: The most recent valuation and rebanding of properties in the UK took place in Wales in 2005. Revaluations are planned for England, Scotland and Northern Ireland in the next few years.)

council tenant *noun* a tenant of a council house

Country Land and Business Association *noun* an organisation representing the interests of landowners (NOTE: Formerly called the 'Country Landowners Association'.)

Countryside Agency *noun* a statutory body funded by Defra with the aim of making life better for people in the countryside

County Borough Council *noun* the local authority of a county borough, a large area administered independently of an administrative county

County Council *noun* a local government body administering a county in the United Kingdom and some parts of the United States, consisting of elected councillors and having responsibilities that include education, police, highways and traffic control, developmental planning and social services

county court *noun* one of the types of court in England and Wales that hears local civil cases

county court judgment *noun* an order to pay money owed, issued by a county court and details of which are held for up to six years on a county court register that can be checked by financial institutions examining a potential customer's credit history. Abbreviation **CCJ**

coupling *noun* a device in a mechanical or electrical system that transfers power from one part to another

court *noun* **1.** a session of an official body that has authority to try cases, resolve disputes or make other legal decisions **2.** a place where a court of law is held **3.** a large open or roofless area within a building **4.** a short street of houses that is closed at one end **5.** a group of houses built around an open space

Court of Session *noun* the highest civil court in Scotland

courtyard garden *noun* a small garden surrounded closely by buildings on several or all sides

covenant *noun* **1.** a solemn agreement that is binding on all parties **2.** a formal and legally binding agreement or contract, e.g. a lease, or a clause in an agreement of this kind (NOTE: A covenant is often used to require an owner or user of a piece of land to do or refrain from doing something.) **3.** a lawsuit for damages that is brought because of the breaking of a legal covenant

covenant to repair *noun* an agreement by a landlord or tenant to keep a rented property in good repair

cowl *noun* a hood-shaped, sometimes revolving, cover fitted to a chimney or vent to improve ventilation and prevent downward draughts

crane *noun* a large machine used to lift and move heavy objects by means of a hook attached to cables suspended from a supporting, usually movable, beam

craneage *noun* cranes and other heavy lifting gear used in the construction industry

crate *noun* a large open sturdy box or basket used to carry or store objects or built to fit and protect something during shipping

credit check *noun* a check of an individual's borrowing and repayment history, undertaken by a financial institution and used for assessing the creditworthiness of a potential customer

credit checking agency *noun* same as **credit reference agency**

credit history *noun* a record of how a potential borrower has repaid his or her previous debts

creditor *noun* a person or organisation owed money by another

credit reference agency *noun* a company that undertakes credit checks for institutions. Also called **credit checking agency**

cribbing *noun* the timbers used for a framework, e.g. of a mineshaft or foundation

critical illness cover *noun* an insurance plan that pays out a guaranteed cash sum if the policyholder is diagnosed as suffering from any of various specified critical illnesses within the term of the plan

croft *noun* a small farm in the Highlands and Islands of Scotland, held subject to the provisions of the Crofters (Scotland) Act 1993

crofter housing grant *noun* a grant awarded by the Scottish Executive to assist crofting

crossbeam *noun* a horizontal beam that is fixed between two vertical supports in the structure of a building

crossover *noun* markings on a pavement which indicate that a vehicle may use it for access, e.g. to a driveway

Crown Court *noun* a court, above the level of the magistrates' courts, that hears criminal cases in England and Wales

Crown Estate *noun* a portfolio of properties associated with the British monarch

Crown Lands *plural noun* land or property belonging to the King or Queen

CSCAE *abbreviation* Consejo Superior de los Colegios de Arquitectos de España

culvert *noun* **1.** a covered channel that carries water or cabling under a road or railway or through an embankment **2.** an arch, bridge or part of a road that covers a culvert

cupola *noun* **1.** a roof or ceiling in the form of a dome **2.** a small structure on a roof, sometimes made of glass and providing natural light inside

currency risk *noun* the risk that the operations of a business or the value of an investment will be affected by changes in exchange rates

current account mortgage *noun* an account that links a mortgage to the operation of a current account, allowing, e.g., a credit in the current account to offset interest on the mortgage

curtain *noun* a piece of cloth hung at a window, in a doorway, or round a bed, usually for privacy or to exclude light or draughts

curtain pole *noun* a support for curtains in the form of a pole over which rings move that hold the curtains

curtain rail, curtain track *noun* a support for curtains in the form of a rail along which curtain fixings slide

curtain wall *noun* an external wall that does not bear any of the load of the building it is attached to

curtilage *noun* land round a house

cut and pitch roof *noun* a pitched roof constructed on site from loose timber, as distinct from a pitched roof constructed from prefabricated trusses

cylinder *noun* a closed container, usually insulated, for storing and supplying domestic hot water

cylinder lock *noun* a traditional type of lock in which the locking mechanism is a cylinder that is rotated

cylinder mortice deadlock *noun* a mortice deadlock with a cylinder action, as distinct from a lever action

D

dado *noun* **1.** the lower part of an interior wall, decorated or faced in a different manner from the upper part, usually with panels, paint or wallpaper **2.** (*in classical architecture*) the part of the pedestal of a column between the base and the cornice **3.** a rectangular groove cut into a board so that a matching piece can be fitted into it to form a joint ■ *verb* **1.** to fit a wall with a dado **2.** to cut a rectangular groove in something so that a matching piece can be fitted into it to form a joint **3.** to insert something into a rectangular groove to form a joint

daily interest *noun* interest calculated on the outstanding balance each day

daily interest mortgage *noun* a mortgage in which daily interest is charged

Dalton's Weekly *noun* a UK magazine listing businesses for sale

damages *plural noun* **1.** money claimed by a claimant from a defendant as compensation for harm done **2.** money awarded by a court as compensation to a claimant

damp *noun* humidity, moisture or slight wetness. ◊ **penetrating damp**, **rising damp**

dampcourse *noun* a layer of waterproof material near the ground in a brick wall that prevents damp from rising

damper *noun* a metal plate that controls the flow of air in a chimney

damp-proof course *noun* same as **dampcourse**

damp-proof membrane *noun* a damp-proofing surface applied to a concrete floor before flooring or carpet is laid

dangerous structure *noun* any structure that could endanger people by its condition, including not only buildings but such things as garden walls, fences and hoardings

Data Protection Act 1998 *noun* a piece of UK legislation introduced to prevent misuse of personal data held on computer

date of entry *noun* (*in Scotland*) the date agreed in the missives on which ownership of the property shall pass from the seller to the purchaser

datum *noun* a point, line or surface used as a basis for measurement or calculation in mapping or surveying

daub *noun* a mixture of clay, lime and chopped straw plastered onto interwoven rods or twigs, known as wattle, to make a wall

deadbolt *noun* a bolt that is operated directly by the turning of a key or knob and not by a spring mechanism

deadlock *noun* a lock that can be opened or closed only with a key

dead weight *noun* a heavy motionless weight bearing down on something or someone

debt *noun* an amount of money, a service or an item of property that is owed to someone

debt consolidation *noun* the practice of replacing several separate loans or sources of debt with a single, theoretically more manageable loan

debt-to-income ratio *noun* the percentage of a person's income that is available for a mortgage payment after all other continuing obligations are met, considered by a lender before approving a home loan

debt transfer *noun* a system in which one lender takes on an existing customer of another lender and assumes his or her debt, usually at a rate of interest that is more attractive to the borrower

Decenel *noun* (*in France*) a type of insurance that gives purchasers of property a guarantee of workmanship for up to ten years

décor *noun* the internal decorations of a property

decorate *verb* to apply paint, wallpaper and other accessories to a room or house

decoration *noun* the application of paint, wallpaper and accessories in a room or house

decorator *noun* **1.** someone whose job is painting and wallpapering houses and other buildings **2.** *US* same as **interior designer**

deed *noun* a signed document that outlines the terms of an agreement, especially one that details a change in ownership of property

deed of assignment *noun* an agreement that legally transfers a property from a debtor to a creditor

deed of conditions *noun* (*in Scotland*) a deed that sets out the conditions that apply to multiple properties in a development of houses or flats

deed of easement *noun* a legal document that sets out the terms of an easement

deed of postponement *noun* an arrangement in which a lender gives its right to first claim on the funds of a housing association to another lender

deed of real burdens *noun* (*in Scotland*) a deed that describes the encumbrances on land constituted in favour of the owner of other land, e.g. A's right of way through B's land benefits A but burdens B

deed of rectification *noun* a document that corrects an error in an existing document relating to ownership of property

deed of substitution *noun* a deed drawn up when a property is converted to a commonhold

deed of variation *noun* a legal document that allows the beneficiaries of a will to change its terms after the death of the testator

deeds release fee *noun* a charge made by a solicitor, conveyancer or estate agent for retrieving a client's deeds from the lender and passing them on to the client

default *verb* to fail to pay a debt or other financial obligation

default notice *noun* a formal document issued by a lender to a borrower who is in default

defect *noun* **1.** a physical problem in a machine, structure or system, especially one that prevents it from functioning correctly **2.** a feature of something that is regarded as inadequate

defective title *noun* a situation in which some aspects of the title deeds are incomplete or faulty

defendant *noun* someone who is sued in a civil case. Compare **claimant**, **plaintiff**

defender *noun* (*in Scotland*) the defendant in a civil case

deferral period *noun* a length of time for which a requirement or obligation is deferred

deferred interest mortgage *noun* a mortgage in which not all of the interest due is paid in the early years

deforce *verb* to take wrongfully and hold land that belongs to someone else

deforcement *noun* the wrongful taking and holding of another person's land

Defra *noun* the Department for Environment, Food and Rural Affairs, a department of the UK government

de minimis *adverb* trivial and not worthy of the attention of the legal profession

demise *noun* 1. death 2. the granting of property on a lease

demolish *verb* 1. to destroy a building or other structure completely, e.g. because it is unsafe or its land is needed for another purpose 2. to damage something so severely that it cannot be repaired or restored

demolition *noun* the complete destruction of a building or other structure, usually because it is unsafe or because its land is needed for something else

demolition contractor *noun* a company that offers demolition services

département *noun* any of the numbered divisions of the country that France is divided into for administrative purposes

Department for Communities and Local Government *noun* a UK government department with responsibility for housing, urban regeneration, planning and local government

dependant *noun* 1. someone who is supported financially by someone else 2. a person who is a member of the family of someone who works in the European Union, even if not a EU citizen

deposit *noun* the proportion of the cost of a property funded directly by the buyer, usually 10% but, with some mortgages, as little as 5% or nothing at all ■ *verb* to pay money into an account in a bank or other financial institution

derate *verb* to lower or abolish the rates on a property

derelict *noun* a building, ship or other property that has been abandoned

dereliction *noun* 1. deliberate neglect of duty or obligations 2. the act of abandoning a building

derelict land *noun* land that has become damaged by industrial or other development

detached *adjective* used for describing a building that stands on its own and is not joined to another building

detail *noun* a small element of the structure of a building, considered separately

develop *verb* 1. to make land available for human purposes, e.g. housing 2. to plan and construct buildings, roads or other technological structures

developer *noun* a person or company that buys land in order to build on it or sell it to others who want to build on it

developer's warranty *noun* a developer's undertaking to carry out any necessary repairs to a new house within the first two years of occupancy

development *noun* a group of houses or other buildings that are built as a single construction project

development area *noun* an area that has been given special help from a government to encourage businesses and factories to be set up there

development plan *noun* a local authority's plans for development in its area

development plan document *noun* a document setting out a local authority's development plan

devisal *noun* the handing down of property through a will

devise *noun* a gift of freehold land to someone in a will ■ *verb* to give freehold property to someone in a will

devisee *noun* someone who receives freehold property in a will

digger *noun* a tool, machine or part of a machine that is used for digging or excavation

dimensions *plural noun* measurements of the size of a property, its buildings or its rooms

dimmer switch *noun* an electrical switch by means of which the level of electrical light in a room can be adjusted gradually

direction départmentale de l'équipement *noun* (*in France*) the planning office in a particular département

disabled facilities grant *noun* a local authority grant to help with the cost of adapting a home for a disabled person

disadvantaged area *noun* **1.** a name for a residential area which is judged to suffer deprivation in one or more areas such as housing, employment, education or skills (NOTE: Property transactions in disadvantaged areas may be subject to tax relief.) **2.** a name for land in mountainous and hilly areas that is capable of improvement and use as breeding and rearing land for sheep and cattle

disbursements *plural noun* costs collected by conveyancing solicitors that are then passed on to a third party, e.g. the Land Registry

discharge fee *noun* a fee charged by a lender at the point when a mortgage is repaid in full, nominally for releasing its charge over a property

discharge of mortgages *noun* the act of paying off a mortgage and obtaining the title deeds from the lender

disclaimer *noun* **1.** a legal refusal to accept responsibility or to accept a right **2.** a clause in a contract in which a party disclaims responsibility for something **3.** a refusal to accept property bequeathed under someone's will

disclaimer of liability *noun* a statement in which an individual or company makes clear that it does not have liability for certain eventualities

disclosure *noun* the revealing of information that was previously kept secret

disconnect *verb* to shut off a telephone line or the supply of water, gas or electricity to a building or customer, which can incur charges

discounted period *noun* a period in a mortgage repayment during which interest rates are lower

discounted variable rate *noun* a variable rate of interest on a mortgage that is lower than the lender's standard variable rate, often offered as an incentive to take up a particular mortgage product

discounted variable rate mortgage *noun* a mortgage to which a discounted variable rate of interest applies

discretionary trust *noun* a trust in which the trustees decide how to invest the income and when and how much income should be paid to the beneficiaries

dishwasher *noun* an electrically operated machine that washes, rinses and dries crockery and kitchen utensils

dispone *verb* (*in Scotland*) to transfer ownership of land from one party to another

disposable income *noun* income that remains available for spending after deductions for taxes, mortgage payments and other obligations

disposition *noun* **1.** the act of passing property in the form of land or goods to another person, especially in a will **2.** (*in Scotland*) the formal deed that conveys property from one party to another

dispositive clause *noun* (*in Scotland*) the effective clause of a deed by which ownership of property is transferred

dispossess *verb* to deprive someone wrongfully of his or her possession of land

dispossession *noun* the act of wrongfully depriving someone of possession of land

dispute *noun* a serious argument or disagreement

dispute resolution *noun* the act of resolving legal disputes

disseisin *noun* the act of illegally depriving someone of possession of land

distribution *noun* the process of sharing out property in an estate

District Council *noun* a division of local government in the UK

divest *verb* to lose or give away rights to the possession of property, or deprive someone of them

DIY *noun* the activity of doing repairs and alterations in the home yourself, especially as a hobby, instead of employing tradespeople to do the work. Full form **do-it-yourself**

DIY conveyancing *noun* conveyancing done by the buyer and seller of a property without professional legal services

DIY financing *noun* the activity of researching and arranging a mortgage without professional advice or services

DIY removal *noun* the practice of carrying out a removal without a professional removals service

do-it-yourself *noun* full form of **DIY**

dome *noun* a hemispherical or convex structure, especially a building

domestic appliance *noun* an appliance such as a cooker or dishwasher that is used in the home

domicile *noun* **1.** someone's true, fixed and legally recognised place of residence, especially in cases of prolonged absence that require him or her to prove a continuing and significant connection with the place **2.** *US* the house, apartment or other place where someone lives (*formal*)

dominant owner *noun* someone who has the right to use someone else's property

dominant tenement *noun* (*in Scotland*) land or property the ownership of which includes a servitude right, e.g. right of access over adjoining land (NOTE: The adjoining land is the **servient tenement**.)

dommage et ouvrage assurance *noun* (*in France*) insurance to cover a property owner in the event that anyone working on his or her property has an accident

door *noun* **1.** a movable barrier used to open and close the entrance to a building, room or cupboard, usually a solid panel hinged to or sliding in a frame **2.** the gap that forms the entrance to a building or room

door closer *noun* a device fitted to a door that closes the door automatically

door handle *noun* a handle fitted to a door and used for opening it

door liner *noun* a kit for making a doorway

door schedule *noun* a document giving details of the location and type of doors in a proposed property

doorstep *noun* a step at the entrance to a building

door stop *noun* **1.** a movable device, e.g. a wedge or heavy object, used to hold a door open **2.** a rubber stud or rubber-tipped projection on a wall, floor or door that prevents damage to the wall when the door is opened

door viewer *noun* a device that allows the person calling at a door to be seen through the door from the inside, designed to protect against potential intruders

doorway *noun* an entrance to a building or room, especially one that has a door

dormant site *noun* an area formerly used for industrial purposes, e.g. quarrying or mining

dormer window *noun* a window that projects from a sloping roof

double bedroom *noun* a bedroom large enough for a double bed

double glazing *noun* windows consisting of two layers of glass separated by a space, designed to provide improved heat and sound insulation

double insurance *noun* a situation in which one person has multiple insurance policies on the same property against identical risks

double taxation *noun* the act of taxing the same income twice

double taxation treaty *noun* a convention between two countries that aims to eliminate the double taxation of income or gains arising in one territory and paid to residents of another territory

dowel bar, dowel rod *noun* a fixing device that holds precast panels in place

downlighter *noun* any light or light fitting designed to cast its light downwards

down pipe *noun* a pipe that carries rainwater from a roof gutter down to a drain or to the ground

downstairs *noun* the lower floor of a building

downturn *noun* the movement of a business or economy towards lower prices, sales or profits

DPC *abbreviation* damp-proof course

DPM *abbreviation* damp-proof membrane

draft contract *noun* a contract that contains details of all provisions and liabilities but not details such as price or cost that are negotiated individually

drain *noun* a pipe or channel that carries water or sewage away from a place

drain, waste, vent *noun* a domestic drainage system that carries wastes away from house fixtures and vents the system above the roof

drainage *noun* **1.** the process of draining liquid from something **2.** a system of pipes or channels that carries water or sewage away from a place

drainage search *noun* a check, made on behalf of a prospective buyer of a property, to establish such information as whether the property is served by public sewers and whether there is a main supply of water

draining board *noun* a slightly sloping metal, wooden, or plastic surface next to a sink, with shallow grooves on it to allow water to drain off drying dishes into the sink

drain shaft *noun* a vertical shaft leading from ground level to an underground sewer or drain

drain test *noun* a test of the efficiency of a system of drains

draught excluder *noun* a device fitted around a door frame or window frame to keep out draughts

draw cord *noun* a device for pulling cables and pipes through ducts

draw down *verb* to request an amount of money offered by a lender but not taken at the outset of the loan

drawdown mortgage *noun* a mortgage in which the full amount of the loan is not taken at the outset but reserved, e.g. for future home improvements

drawing room *noun* traditionally, a room in a house in which guests are entertained

dressing room *noun* a small room in which clothes are stored, where people get dressed or change their clothes

drill *noun* a tool or machine that bores holes

drill bit *noun* a tool that fits into a drill and forms the drilling edge

drive, driveway *noun* a paved or surfaced area or private road that goes between a house or garage and the street

droits de donations *noun* (*in France*) gift tax

droits de succession *noun* (*in France*) inheritance tax

drop kerb *noun* a kerb, of the kind installed at the entrance to a driveway, that drops to the level of the road to allow vehicles to drive over

drove *noun* a broad-edged chisel used for dressing stone

dry lining *noun* the construction of interior walls using a product such as plasterboard, as distinct from the application of wet plaster to brickwork or blockwork

dry rot *noun* dry crumbling decay in wood caused by various fungi

drywall *noun US* **1.** same as **plasterboard 2.** a wall constructed with sheets of plasterboard

duct *noun* a tube or channel through which something such as air flows or something such as a pipe or cable is laid ■ *verb* to supply or equip something such as a building with a duct or a system of ducts

ducting *noun* **1.** a duct or system of ducts **2.** materials that can be used as ducts

dust sheet *noun* a large piece of cloth placed over furniture or furnishings to protect them from dust, dirt or paint

duty of disclosure *noun* a seller's duty to disclose important information relating to a property, e.g. the presence of lead piping

E

EA *abbreviation* Environment Agency

early redemption charge *noun* a fee charged by a lender in the event that a mortgage is repaid in full before the agreed term

earthmoving equipment *noun* heavy machinery and vehicles designed to move large quantities of earth, used on major construction projects

easement *noun* a right that someone has to make use of land belonging to someone else for a purpose such as a path (NOTE: The most well-known easement is a 'right of way', where it is necessary to use a neighbour's land to access one's own property, but others include 'right to light' (a person may not build a structure on their own land which blocks the light to a neighbouring property) and 'right of support' (a person may not remove structures on their own land which support a neighbour's building, such as with a semi-detached house).)

Economy 7 *noun* a system in which domestic hot water is heated using electricity on an 'off-peak' tariff

e-conveyancing *noun* same as **electronic transfer**

edge bead *noun* a metal trim that covers the exposed edge of a plasterboard wall

EDM *abbreviation* electronic distance measurer

efflorescence *noun* a powdery substance that forms on the surface of rocks and brickwork

effluent tank *noun* any tank that stores effluent such as domestic sewage or industrial waste

eggshell *adjective* used for describing paint that has a slight sheen, with a finish between that of gloss and matt paint

egress window *noun* a window through which the occupants of a building can safely escape in the event of an emergency

EH *abbreviation* English Heritage

EIA *abbreviation* environmental impact assessment

eject *verb* to make someone leave a property that he or she is occupying illegally

ejection *noun* the action of making someone leave a property that he or she is occupying illegally

elbow *noun* **1.** a bend in something such as a road or pipe **2.** something, especially a piece of pipe, made with a bend in it

electoral register, electoral roll *noun* a register, kept by a local authority, of names of people who are eligible to vote in local and national elections

Electrical Contractors' Association *noun* a UK trade association that promotes good practice and provides training in all aspects of electrical installation

electrical test screwdriver *noun* an insulated screwdriver that indicates whether a wire or device touched by the tip is connected to mains electricity

electricity meter *noun* a device installed inside or outside a building which measures the amount of something being used, such as gas, electricity or water

electronic distance measurer *noun* any of various devices that measure distance by means of sound waves. Abbreviation **EDM**

electronic transfer *noun* the transfer of interests in land by electronic methods rather than paper documents

elevation *noun* **1.** the height above a specific reference point, especially sea level **2.** a scale drawing of any side of a building or other structure **3.** the angle between a horizontal line and the line from a surveying instrument to a point above the horizontal, e.g. between eye level and a line to a nearby rooftop

Elizabethan *adjective* dating from, or built in a style of English Renaissance building from, the reign of Elizabeth I that emphasised symmetrical layouts and moulded or sculptured decoration with a German or Flemish influence

embrasure *noun* an opening in the wall of a building for a door or window, tapered so as to be wider on the inside than on the outside

eminent domain *noun* the right of the state to appropriate private property for public use

employer's reference *noun* a written statement from an employer confirming the borrower's employment, giving details of his or her salary, status of the employment e.g. permanent, part time or contract, and length of service

empty property *noun* a property that is currently unoccupied, subject to a lower rate of council tax or business rate

emulsion *noun* a water-based paint used for interior decorating, usually with a matt or silk finish

EN *abbreviation* Europaische Norm

enclosure *noun* **1.** a document enclosed with a letter **2.** the act of removing land from common use by putting fences round it

encumbrance *noun* a charge or claim on property, especially a mortgage

endowment *noun* an amount of income or property that has been provided to a person or institution, especially an educational institution

endowment mortgage *noun* a mortgage backed by an endowment policy (NOTE: Very popular in the 1980s and 90s, when interest rates were relatively high, endowment mortgages have become less popular owing to the relatively low rate of return on investments and the increased likelihood of the borrower being left with a shortfall, and owing to controversy aroused by claims made by many policyholders that potential shortfall was not fully explained to them and that the products were consequently missold.)

endowment mortgage compensation *noun* compensation paid to the holder of an endowment mortgage that was missold to them

endowment shortfall *noun* the amount by which the final value of an endowment policy falls short of the amount of the mortgage, leaving the mortgage holder with a debt

energy efficiency assessment *noun* an assessment of the cost of heating the space and water in a home, using the UK government's standard assessment procedure

energy management system *noun* a computer-based system that monitors energy consumption in a building or on a site

energy performance certificate *noun* an official record of a home's energy efficiency assessment, to be included in a Home Information Pack

Energywatch *noun* the UK's independent gas and electricity consumer watchdog

enforcement notice *noun* a notice issued by a local planning authority which outlines the steps that need to be taken within a specified time to stop or repair a breach of planning control

English Heritage *noun* an organisation partly funded by government that is responsible for maintaining buildings and monuments of historical interest in England. Abbreviation **EH**

English Partnerships *plural noun* a UK agency that advises the government on the development of many aspects of the built environment

engrossment *noun* **1.** the process of drawing up of a legal document in its final form **2.** a legal document in its final form

en indivision *adjective* (*in France*) a form of property ownership when buying with a partner

en suite *noun* a bathroom leading off a bedroom (*informal*) ■ *adjective* used for describing a bathroom that leads off a bedroom

entail *noun* **1.** the limiting of the future ownership of bequeathed property to particular descendants **2.** a property that has been entailed ■ *verb* to restrict the future ownership of property to particular descendants, through instructions written into a will

en tontine *adjective* (*in France*) a form of property ownership when buying with a partner, similar to a joint tenancy in the UK

entry date *noun* same as **date of entry**

Environment Agency *noun* (*in England and Wales*) the government agency responsible for protection of the environment, including flood and sea defences. Abbreviation **EA**

environmental health department *noun* a local authority department responsible for improving the quality of the environment and protecting public health and safety

environmental impact assessment *noun* an evaluation of the effect on the environment of an action such as a large construction programme. Abbreviation **EIA**

environmental impairment cover *noun* insurance that covers against liability for sudden and unforeseen pollution emanating from a particular property or site

Environmental Protection Act *noun* a piece of UK legislation that sought to control the environmental impact of various practices and substances. Abbreviation **EPA**

environmental search *noun* a check, made on behalf of a prospective buyer of a property, to establish such information as whether the property is at risk from flooding or industrial pollution

EPA *abbreviation* Environmental Protection Act

epigraph *noun* an inscription on something such as a statue or building

epitome of title *noun* a set of documents compiled to establish the ownership of unregistered land

Equifax *noun* a major credit reference agency

equitable *adjective* applicable under the law of equity as distinguished from common or statute law

equitable interests *plural noun* interests in property that are recognised separately from rights given by law

equitable lien *noun* a right of someone to hold property that legally he or she does not own until the owner pays money due

equitable mortgage *noun* a mortgage that does not give the mortgagee a legal estate in the land mortgaged

equitable owner *noun* the beneficiary of a property that is held in trust

equity *noun* the value of a piece of property over and above any mortgage or other liabilities relating to it

equity appreciation *noun* an increase in the value of property that someone owns

equity depreciation *noun* a decrease in the value of property that someone owns

equity of redemption *noun* the right of a mortgagor to redeem the estate by paying off the principal and interest

equity release plan *noun* a scheme under which an institution pays a lump sum in return for a share of the ownership of a property after the owner's death

erect *verb* to build a structure from basic parts and materials

erection *noun* **1.** the construction or setting up of something **2.** something that has been built or constructed (*formal*)

erector *noun* someone who erects buildings and other structures

erosion *noun* the gradual wearing away of rock or soil by physical breakdown, chemical solution and transportation of material, as caused, e.g., by water, wind or ice

escritura de compraventa *noun* (*in Spain*) a deed of purchase and sale or a deed of conveyance

escritura pública de compra e venda *noun* (*in Portugal*) a deed of purchase and sale

escutcheon *noun* a plate or shield fixed around something such as a light switch or keyhole, as an ornament or to protect the surrounding surface

established use *noun* the use of land for a specific purpose that is recognised by a local authority because the land has been used for this purpose for some time

estate *noun* **1.** an interest in or right to hold and occupy land **2.** all the property that is owned by a person, especially a person who has recently died

estate agency *noun* an office that arranges for the sale and purchase of properties

estate agency fees *plural noun* fees paid by a property buyer or seller in return for services provided by an estate agent (NOTE: The average commission charged by an estate agents on a sale is 2–3% of the property's value.)

estate agent *noun* a person who is qualified to arrange the sale and purchase of property

Estate Agents Act 1979 *noun* a piece of UK legislation designed to ensure that estate agents act fairly towards clients

Estate Agents (Account) Regulations *plural noun* regulations stating that estate agents must hold clients' money, e.g. deposits on houses, in a separate and dedicated bank account

Estate Agents (Provision of Information) Regulations *plural noun* regulations governing the information that estate agents are required to give both to sellers and prospective buyers of property

estate duty *noun US* a tax paid on the property left by a dead person

Estates Gazette *noun* a weekly guide to the UK commercial property industry

estimate *noun* an assessment of the likely price of something such as an item to be bought or a job to be done

estimator *noun* a person whose job is to calculate estimates for carrying out work

ethical mortgage *noun* a mortgage from a lender that proclaims its investment or its lending policies to be 'ethical' to a degree

Europaische Norm *noun* the European equivalent of the British Standard. Abbreviation **EN**

European Builders Confederation *noun* a group of national building federations representing small and medium-sized building businesses among the member states of the European Union and Switzerland

European Confederation of Real Estate Agents *noun* a professional organisation of estate agents established with the purpose of improving international cooperation, advising on issues concerning transnational real estate transactions and influencing European ruling where this relates to real estate practice

evict *verb* to force someone, especially a tenant, to leave a property

eviction *noun* the act of forcing someone, especially a tenant, to leave a property

evidence of title *noun* a document that provides proof of ownership of property

excavator *noun* a large machine with a hinged metal bucket attached to a hydraulic arm, used for moving large quantities of earth or soil or for lifting

excess *noun* a particular amount of money that a policyholder must pay towards the cost of any insurance claim made

exchange *verb* to sign a contract with the seller before buying something, e.g. a house

Exchange and Mart *noun* a magazine and website listing several classes of item for sale, including properties

exchange of contracts *noun* a point in the conveyance of a property when the solicitors for the buyer and seller hand over the contract of sale which then becomes binding

excluded from sale *adjective* used for describing items not included in a sale of land or property

excluded tenancy *noun* a tenancy that operates in the case of someone renting out a room or other part of his or her home

excluder *noun* same as **draught excluder**

exclusion clause *noun* a clause in an insurance policy or contract stating which items are not covered by the policy and giving details of circumstances in which the insurance company will refuse to pay

excrescence *noun* an ugly addition or extension to something such as a building

exedra *noun* **1.** a long curved or semicircular outdoor bench, usually with a high back **2.** a recess or niche (*technical*)

existing liabilities *plural noun* long-term debts such as hire purchase agreements and personal loans, considered by a lender when assessing whether or not to offer a mortgage

ex-local authority *adjective* used for describing a property that used to be owned by a local authority but is now privately owned (NOTE: Ex-local flats as part of a block will usually be sold leasehold, with the council retaining freeholder status.)

Expamet *noun* expanded metal used as a construction material

expansion tank *noun* a storage tank for domestic hot water that allows for the expansion of water owing to heating and reduces the risk of a dangerous build-up of water pressure

Experian *noun* a business information company providing a range of services, including credit reference

expert immobilier *noun* (*in France*) a professional broadly equivalent to a surveyor

expertise *noun* specialist knowledge or skill in a particular field

express term *noun* a term in a contract that is agreed by both parties and clearly stated. Compare **implied term**

expropriation *noun* **1.** the action of the state in taking private property for public use without paying compensation **2.** *US* same as **compulsory purchase**

extended redemption penalty *noun* a penalty fee, similar to an early redemption charge, payable if the mortgage is paid off in full within a specified period following the end of any special deal that existed at the time of taking out the mortgage

extended tie-in *noun* a situation in which a borrower cannot switch mortgage lenders even after a period of preferential interest rates has ended

extension *noun* **1.** a room or area added to an existing building **2.** same as **extension lead**

extension lead *noun* a lead with a plug at one end and one or more sockets at the other, plugged into the mains to provide a power supply remote from the wall socket

extent *noun* **1.** the area or range covered or affected by something **2.** a writ that authorises someone to take possession of the property of a person who owes him or her money

external *adjective* situated on, happening on, or coming from the outside

external door *noun* a door that leads to the outside

external wall structure *noun* the type of construction of an external wall, e.g. a timber-frame and cavity-wall construction or a solid-stone construction

extinguishment (of easement) *noun* the termination of an easement

extractor fan *noun* an electric fan, often set into a window, used to remove steam, fumes, or stale air from a room or building

extractor hood *noun* a kitchen fixture fitted over a cooking area to vent cooking smells and gases to the outside

eyeball light *noun* a wall- or ceiling-mounted light that swivels within a socket, allowing for numerous lighting positions

eyehole *noun* a small hole in a door or wall, for looking through

eye-level unit *noun* a kitchen unit fitted at eye level

F

fabric *noun* the material from which something is constructed, especially a building, or the physical structure of something

fabrication *noun* the construction of something, or something that has been constructed or made

fabricator *noun* a company that manufactures structural parts from a particular material, e.g. steel

facade *noun* the face of a building, especially the principal or front face showing its most prominent architectural features

face *noun* the exterior of the front or side of a large building ■ *verb* **1.** to be positioned or turn so that the front side is directed a particular way or towards something **2.** to put a smooth surface on a piece of stone

faceplate *noun* a plate that houses a light switch or similar control, fitted to a wall

facing *noun* a layer of material that covers the outer surface of a wall to decorate or protect it

factor *noun* (*in Scotland*) a person or company that manages an estate or large property on behalf of the owner ■ *verb* (*in Scotland*) to manage an estate or property on behalf of the owner

factoring *noun* (*in Scotland*) the activity of managing credit and debt collections in relation to an estate or large property

factor's charges *plural noun* (*in Scotland*) payments charged by factor for his or her services

fair price *noun* a good price for both buyer and seller

fair rent *noun* reasonable rent for a property, bearing in mind the size and type of property and its situation

fair rent review *noun* a rent review that seeks to establish a new fair rent

fair value *noun* a price that both buyer and seller are aware is fair

family room *noun* a room in a house for relaxing in

fan *noun* a device that circulates currents of air to keep a room cool, especially one with rotating blades

farm diversification *noun* the use of farmland for alternative business ventures, e.g. for leisure activities, tourist accommodation or the generation of alternative power

farmhouse *noun* a house on a farm, especially the main dwelling place of the farmer

farmhouse sink *noun* a type of sink basin which is formed from a carved block of stone, or a piece of shaped metal or plastic resembling this

fascia *noun* the flat horizontal surface immediately below the edge of a roof

feature *noun* an aspect of a property that is a special attraction, e.g. a particularly attractive fixture such as a fireplace

Federation of European Moving Associations *noun* an umbrella organisation that coordinates efforts of national associations at a European level

Federation of International Furniture Removers *noun* an international association that certifies removal companies

Federation of Master Builders *noun* a UK trade association established to protect the interests of small and medium-sized building firms

Federation of Overseas Property Developers, Agents and Consultants *noun* an association established to unite those agents, developers and specialist consultants active in the international property markets

Federation of Plastering and Drywall Contractors *noun* a UK employers' organisation for the plastering and drywall industry

Federation of Private Residents' Associations *noun* a UK organisation that provides advice and information for subscribing residents' associations and collectively owned freehold blocks of flats

fee *noun* **1.** a payment for professional services **2.** (*in Scotland*) a right to land that can be passed on by inheritance

fee indemnity guarantee premium *noun* an insurance premium that insures a lender against any loss of money, e.g. if the borrower defaults on the loan

fee simple *noun* freehold ownership of land with no restrictions to it. Also called **freehold absolute**

felt *noun* a synthetic fabric made by the process of matting, especially a heavy paper permeated with asphalt, used as a roof sealant

female socket *noun* a standard socket, with holes for the pins of a male plug to fit into

fence *noun* a structure erected to enclose an area and act as a barrier, especially one made of wood or with posts and wire ■ *verb* to enclose an area or bar a gap by erecting a fence

fence post *noun* a vertical post that supports a fence, fixed into the ground or to a building

fencing *noun* materials used in making fences, e.g. posts and wire

fenestra *noun* a window or similar opening on the outer wall of a building

fenestration *noun* the design and placing of windows in a building

festoon *noun* a carved representation of a festoon in the masonry of a building

feu *noun* 1. (*in Scotland*) a right to use land or property in return for an annual payment called feu duty 2. (*in Scotland*) a form of land tenure in feudal times, based on paying rent in money or grain and not on military service 3. (*in Scotland*) a piece of land held by feu

feudal ownership *noun* (*in Scotland*) the system of landholding that existed until 2004, in which, in principle, the sovereign owned the land. Also called **feuhold**

feu disposition *noun* (*in Scotland*) under the feudal system, a document that established feudal ownership

feu duty *noun* (*in Scotland*) an annual payment made by the owner of a building to the nominal feudal superior for the right to use the land or property

feuhold *noun* same as **feudal ownership**

fibreglass *noun* a lightweight hard structural material made from glass fibres

fibreglass reinforced plastic *noun* same as **glass reinforced plastic**

fibremesh *noun* a product, widely used in civil engineering projects, in the form of a lightweight, high strength synthetic mesh interwoven to form a grid construction, coated with PVC and fire retardants

fibre reinforced concrete *noun* concrete with polypropylene or steel fibres uniformly distributed throughout the mix to increase durability and toughness

fiduciary *adjective* acting as trustee for someone else, or being in a position of trust

filament *noun* a thin wire that produces light in an incandescent bulb when electricity passes through it

filler *noun* a substance used to plug a crack or cavity or smooth a surface

final sale price *noun* the price for which a property is finally sold, after all negotiations over price are complete

financial institution *noun* a bank, investment trust or insurance company whose work involves lending or investing large sums of money

financial relief *noun* any or all of the following orders available during family proceedings: maintenance pending suit orders, financial provision orders, property adjustment orders and court orders for maintenance during marriage

Financial Services Authority *noun* an independent non-governmental body formed in 1997 as a result of reforms in the regulation of financial services in the United Kingdom. Abbreviation **FSA**

Financial Services Compensation Scheme *noun* the UK's statutory fund of last resort for customers of financial services firms, providing compensation to consumers if a financial services firm is unable, or likely to be unable, to pay claims against it

finca rustica *noun* (*in Spain*) rural land

finca urbana *noun* (*in Spain*) urban land, or land that is predominantly built up

finder's fee *noun* a fee paid to a person who finds a client for another

finial *noun* **1.** a carved decoration at the top of a gable, spire or arched structure **2.** an ornamental feature on the top or end of an object such as a piece of furniture, stair post or curtain rail, e.g. a carved knob

finish *verb* to treat something, especially wood or metal, in order to achieve a desired surface effect

fire alarm *noun* a bell that rings if there is a fire

fire certificate *noun* a document issued by a municipal fire department to say that a building is properly protected against fire

fire damage *noun* damage to land caused by a fire

fire door *noun* a special door designed to prevent fire going from one part of a building to another

fire extinguisher *noun* a portable device, usually painted red, for putting out fires

fireguard *noun* a metal, usually meshed screen that is put around the front of an open fire, mainly to stop sparks from flying out and to prevent people from going too close. Also called **firescreen**

fire hazard *noun* a situation, or a set of materials, that could easily start a fire or could burn easily or dangerously

fireplace *noun* a recess, usually with a mantelpiece above it, built into the wall of a room as a place to light an open fire

fire plan *noun* an overall plan at design stage for how a building will be protected against fire. Also called **fire strategy**

fire protection system *noun* a system that protects a building against fire, comprising a range of devices that may include sprinklers, smoke control and stair pressurisation

fire regulations *plural noun* local or national regulations that owners of buildings used by the public have to obey in order to be granted a fire certificate

firescreen *noun* same as **fireguard**

fire stop *adjective* used for describing systems and products designed to prevent the spread of fire in a building

fire strategy *noun* same as **fire plan**

first legal charge *noun* a lender's overriding right to receive any funds available from the sale of the property

first time buyer *noun* someone who is buying a house for the first time. Abbreviation **FTB**

fit for habitation *adjective* satisfying the basic requirement of being safe and healthy enough to live in

fitting *noun* a detachable part, especially for a device or machine. ◊ **fixtures and fittings**

fixed capital *noun* capital in the form of buildings and machinery

fixed charge *noun* a charge over a particular asset or property

fixed fee *adjective* a flat rate charged by some lenders for arranging a mortgage, as distinct from a fee linked to the price of the property

fixed fee conveyancing *noun* conveyancing services performed in return for a flat-rate payment, as distinct from a payment linked to the cost of the property

fixed price *noun* (*in Scotland*) a single price that a seller of property will accept, rather than a price above which offers are invited

fixed rate *noun* a charge for services that cannot be negotiated

fixed rate mortgage *noun* a mortgage with an interest rate that will remain at a specified level for the term of the loan

fixed term tenancy *noun* a tenancy that operates for a specified period

fixings *plural noun* items such as screws, nails and bolts

fixture *noun* an item such as a sink or lavatory that is permanently attached to a property and passes to a new owner with the property itself

fixtures, fittings and contents form *noun* a form that constitutes a definitive statement of what is and is not included in the sale price of a property

fixtures and fittings *plural noun* objects in a property that are sold with the property, including both objects that are permanently fixed, e.g. fireplaces, and those that can be removed relatively easily, e.g. curtain poles

flag *verb* to pave a surface with flagstones

flagstone *noun* a slab of stone or concrete used for making floors or paving

flakeboard *noun* a cheap board composed of large flakes of wood glued together to form a thick layer of shavings, often used for loft flooring and roof lining

flange *noun* a projecting collar, rim, or rib on an object for fixing it to another object, holding it in place, or strengthening it (NOTE: Flanges are often found on pipes and shafts.)

flange joint *noun* a joint, e.g. between pipes, in which sections are joined by means of projecting edges or flanges bolted together

flash *verb* to fix flashing to a part of a roof or window

flashing *noun* strips of sheet metal, usually lead or aluminium, fitted on a roof, e.g. on the ridge of a slate roof, or around a window frame to provide a waterproof seal

flat *noun* living quarters in part of a building, usually on one floor

flat-pack furniture *noun* furniture bought in sections that the buyer has to assemble

flat plate *adjective* used for describing a fixture such as light switch that is designed to be more or less flush to the surface it is fitted to

flat roof *noun* a roof consisting of a single surface that is more or less parallel with the ground, as distinct from a pitched roof

flier *noun* a rectangular step in a straight flight of stairs

flight *noun* a group of stairs that go from one level of a building to another

float *noun* **1.** a tool with a handle and flat rectangular blade for applying plaster to a wall **2.** a hollow ball that forms part of a ballcock, designed to rest on the water level in a tank to regulate the flow of water

floating charge *noun* a charge under a mortgage agreement linked to any of the person's assets in a category, but not to any specific item

floating floor *noun* a floor that is laid on top of underlay and is not glued or nailed to the permanent floor

floating rate *noun* same as **variable rate**

flood plain *noun* a wide flat part of the bottom of a valley that is usually covered with water when the river floods

flood risk *noun* the risk that a property will be damaged by flooding

flood risk assessment *noun* an assessment of how a property will be protected against potential flooding, provided by a specialist company and often required before planning permission is granted in areas regarded by the Environment Agency as being at risk of flooding

floorboard *noun* one of the strips of wood that are used to make a wood floor

floor covering *noun* material for covering floor surfaces, e.g. carpeting, or a carpet or mat made from such a material

floor hatch *noun* a hatch built into a floor to allow access to underfloor structures such as pipes, timbers and wiring

floor insulation *noun* any of various products designed to prevent heat in a building from escaping through floors or draughts from entering through floors

floorplan *noun* a plan of a room or floor of a building drawn to scale as if viewed from above

flue *noun* a shaft, tube, or pipe used as an outlet to carry smoke, gas, or heat, e.g. from a fireplace or furnace

flue damper *noun* a vent in a chimney that reduces the wasteful removal of warm air from the room and also controls the burn rate of the fire

flue lining *noun* any of various materials used for lining a flue to prevent fumes and tar from leaching into walls, traditionally lime and clay but now often a flexible metal tube

fluorescent lighting *noun* lighting by means of tubes filled with a vapour that gives off light

flush *adjective* completely level so as to form an even surface

flush valve *noun* a valve in a cistern that controls the flow of water, usually into a toilet bowl

flying freehold *noun* a section of a freehold property that is structurally above another person's property

fly tipper *noun* someone who engages in fly tipping

fly tipping *noun* the illegal depositing of rubbish in an unauthorised place

folly *noun* a building of eccentric or overelaborate design, usually built for decorative rather than practical purposes

footing *noun* the foundation or base of a structure such as a wall or column

forcible entry *noun* formerly, the criminal offence of entering a building or land and taking possession of it by force

foreclose *verb* to take possession of a property because the owner cannot repay money that he or she has borrowed using the property as security

foreclosure *noun* the act of foreclosing

foreclosure order absolute *noun* a court order giving the mortgage lender full rights to the property

foreclosure order nisi *noun* a court order that makes a mortgagor pay outstanding debts to a mortgage lender within a specified period of time

foreign currency mortgage *noun* a mortgage denominated in a foreign currency, which sometimes brings advantages relating to interest rates and exchange rates

foreman *noun* a man who is in charge of a group of other workers, e.g. on a building site

foreperson *noun* a skilled worker who is in charge of a group of other workers, e.g. on a building site

foresight *noun* (*in surveying*) an observation or measurement made looking forwards

Forestry Commission *noun* a UK government agency responsible for the management of state-owned forests

forfeiture *noun* the act of forfeiting a property or a right

forfeiture of lease *noun* a situation in which a landlord retakes possession of a property following a tenant's failure to remedy some breach of the lease that occurred earlier

formal written offer *noun* (*in Scotland*) a document, prepared by a solicitor or conveyancer, that constitutes an offer to buy property

Formica a trade name for a strong plastic laminate sheeting that is durable and easy to clean, often used for covering work surfaces

for sale board *noun* a board carrying an announcement that a property is for sale, placed on or in the grounds of the property

fortify *verb* to strengthen or reinforce the structure of something

forward *adjective* to send on mail from the address to which it was originally sent ■ *adverb* used for describing procedures relating to property that take place before the construction of the property has been completed

fossil fuel *noun* any of various natural substances containing carbon formed from the decomposed remains of prehistoric plants, e.g. oil, natural gas or peat

foul drain *noun* a drain that carries toilet waste from a building

foul water *noun* water containing waste or sewage

foundation *noun* a part of a building, usually below the ground, that transfers and distributes the weight of the building onto the ground

foundation stone *noun* a stone laid during a ceremony to mark the start of construction of a building or institution

foundation tie *noun* a beam or similar structural component that connects the foundation of a building to the ground or is braced against the ground

foyer *noun* **1.** the reception area in a public building such as a hotel or theatre **2.** *US* the entrance hall or vestibule in a private house

fraud *noun* the crime of obtaining property or money from someone after making him or her believe something that is not true

fraudulent conveyance *noun* an act of putting a property into someone else's possession to avoid it being seized to pay creditors

freehold *noun* the absolute right to hold land or property for an unlimited time without paying rent

freehold absolute *noun* same as **fee simple**

freeholder *noun* someone who holds a freehold property

freehold flat *noun* a flat the owner of which also has the freehold on the land on which it is built

freehold possessory *noun* a type of freehold in which a third party may have some claim on ownership

freehold property *noun* property that the owner holds in freehold

freehold qualified *noun* a form of ownership of property in which the land registrar considers that the applicant's title to the property can only be established for a limited period, because of past irregularities

freestanding furniture *noun* furniture that is not built into a room and may be moved about freely

freestone *noun* a variety of masonry stone that has a uniform texture and can be chiselled without breaking or splitting, e.g. limestone or fine sandstone

free valuation *noun* an estate agent's valuation of a property for which no fee is charged

french windows *plural noun* tall windows that reach to the floor and can be opened like doors

FRICS *abbreviation* Fellow of the Royal Institution of Chartered Surveyors

frieze *noun* **1.** a band of decoration running along the wall of a room, usually just below the ceiling **2.** (*in classical architecture*) a horizontal band forming part of the entablature, situated between the architrave and the cornice and often decorated with sculpted ornaments or figures

front *noun* a facade of a building, especially the one that faces the street ■ *verb* to give something a visible surface of a particular kind

frontage *noun* **1.** the front side of a building or piece of property **2.** the land between a building and a street or road **3.** the length of the front of a building or piece of land next to a street, river or lake **4.** a piece of land situated next to a street, river or lake **5.** the direction in which a building faces

frontager *noun* the owner of any property or land that abuts or adjoins the street

front door *noun* the main entrance to a house or other building, closed by a door

frontispiece *noun* **1.** the principal facade of a building, treated architecturally as a separate element **2.** a pediment, usually ornamental, above a window or door

FRP *abbreviation* fibreglass reinforced plastic

FSA *abbreviation* Financial Services Authority

FTB *abbreviation* first time buyer

full repairing lease *noun* a lease in which where the tenant has to pay for all repairs to the property

full status mortgage *noun* a mortgage for which a credit check is carried out on the applicant

full structural survey *noun* a survey that involves an extensive investigation of the property and a thorough examination of all the major aspects and minor details that are visible

full title guarantee *noun* a seller's guarantee that he or she has the power to sell a property and also that it is being sold free from any charges, encumbrances or adverse rights

furnished *adjective* containing or supplied with furniture

furnishings *noun* articles of furniture and other useful or decorative items for a room, e.g. carpets and curtains

furniture *noun* **1.** the movable items in a room, e.g. chairs, desks and cabinets **2.** the metal or plastic accessories fitted to an item of joinery or cabinetwork, e.g. door hinges and drawer handles

Furniture Re-use Network *noun* a national body that supports, assists and develops charitable organisations involved in re-using furniture across the UK

furring *noun* **1.** the placing of strips of wood, metal or brick across the studs or joists in a building to create a firm and level foundation for plaster, flooring or another surface **2.** strips used in a building for furring

further advance *noun* an additional sum of money loaned under the terms of an existing mortgage

fuse *noun* an electrical safety device containing a piece of a metal that melts if the current running through it exceeds a particular level, thereby breaking the circuit

fusebox *noun* a box, often a cupboard fitted to a wall, that contains the fuses that protect all the electrical circuits in a building or part of a building

future interest *noun* an interest in property that will be enjoyed in the future (NOTE: Formerly called **future estate**.)

G

gable *noun* **1.** the triangular top section of a side wall on a building with a pitched roof that fills the space beneath where the roof slopes meet **2.** same as **gable end 3.** a triangular structure added to a building for decoration, e.g. a canopy over a door or window

gable end *noun* the end of a building above which there is a gable

gallery *noun* **1.** a balcony or passage running along the wall of a large building **2.** a corridor, hall or other enclosed passageway inside a building **3.** a long narrow space or room used for a particular purpose **4.** a long covered passageway that is open on one or both sides **5.** a decorative metal or wooden rail on a table top, shelf or tray

galvanised steel *noun* mild steel with a coating of zinc, widely used as a structural material

garage *noun* a building for parking or storing one or more motor vehicles

garden *noun* an area of ground adjacent to a building, in which plants are typically grown, used for relaxation, leisure and possibly horticulture ■ *adjective* relating to, produced in or used in a garden

garden shed *noun* a small outbuilding, usually made of wood, erected in a garden for use as storage

garnishment *noun* a legal summons or warning concerning the taking of a debtor's property or wages to satisfy a debt

gas appliance *noun* any appliance that uses gas as fuel, e.g. a gas fire or gas cooker

gas engineer *noun* someone who installs and repairs gas appliances

gasket *noun* a piece of material, often a rubber or paper disc, used for sealing a joint between objects, e.g. pipes

gas meter *noun* a device installed inside or outside a residential or commercial building to measure the amount of gas consumed in a specific period

Gas Safety (Installation and Use) Regulations *noun* regulations that place specific duties on gas engineers, landlords and suppliers of gas services

gate *noun* **1.** a movable barrier, usually on hinges, that closes a gap in a fence or wall **2.** an opening in a wall or fence

gate valve *noun* a valve that opens by lifting a round or rectangular wedge out of the path of the fluid

gauge *noun* **1.** a device or instrument for measuring an amount or quantity or for testing accuracy **2.** the diameter of something, especially of wire or a needle **3.** the proportion of plaster of Paris that is added to mortar to speed up the setting of the mixture

gazebo *noun* **1.** a small, usually open-sided and slightly elevated building situated in a spot that commands a pleasant view **2.** a lightweight freestanding open-sided canopy for use in a garden, usually as a sunshade

gazump *verb* to reject a previously agreed offer to buy a property after receiving a better offer from another buyer

gazundering *noun* the unscrupulous practice of forcing a seller into accepting a lower offer for his or her property just before contracts are exchanged, using the threat of pulling out of the purchase completely

gearing *noun* the act of borrowing money, at fixed interest, that is then invested to yield more profit than the interest paid

general lien *noun* the holding of goods or property until a debt has been paid

General Register of Sasines *noun* (*in Scotland*) a record of all transfers of ownership of property. Also called **Sasine Register**

gentleman's agreement, gentlemen's agreement *noun* a verbal agreement between two parties who trust each other (NOTE: A gentleman's agreement is not usually enforceable by law.)

genuine purchaser *noun* someone who is really interested in buying a property

geometra *noun* (*in Italy*) an architect

géomètre *noun* (*in France*) a land surveyor

Georgian *adjective* built in or imitating a neoclassical style of architecture or furniture that flourished in Great Britain and the United States in the 18th and early 19th centuries

geotextiles *plural noun* permeable fabrics used for structures installed in the ground, e.g. in drainage and filtration systems

gestor *noun* (*in Spain and Portugal*) a professional who acts as an intermediary between people and the state, e.g. when needing assistance to complete a tax return or purchase a property

Gestores Intermediarios en Promociones de Edificaciones *plural noun* (*in Spain*) a body that regulates estate agency. Abbreviation **GIPE**

gift tax *noun* a tax on gifts. Only gifts between husband and wife are exempt.

gimlet *noun* a small tool for boring holes in wood, consisting of a slim metal rod with a sharp corkscrew end, fitted in a handle at a right angle

GIPE *abbreviation* Gestores Intermediarios en Promociones de Edificaciones

Glass and Glazing Federation *noun* a trade association for all companies who make, supply or fit flat glass

glass block *noun* a translucent block of glass used for building partitions in spaces where loss of natural light is to be avoided

glasspaper *noun* an abrasive substance with a rough surface formed of glass particles, used for smoothing wood

glass reinforced plastic *noun* a construction material consisting of plastic reinforced with fibreglass. Abbreviation **GRP**

glasswork *noun* **1.** the technique or result of cutting and fitting glass, especially glass panes for windows, doors and conservatories **2.** glass panes in windows, doors and conservatories

glaze *verb* to fit glass into something, especially a window or door

glazing *noun* **1.** glass in general, especially the type of glass used in windows or doors **2.** the process of fitting glass into windows and doors

gloss *noun* used for describing paint that has a high sheen, shinier than eggshell or matt paint ■ *verb* to apply gloss paint to something

going concern *noun* a company that is actively trading and making a profit

good leasehold *noun* a leasehold title that is equivalent to an absolute title but for the fact that it cannot be guaranteed that a landlord will grant a lease

goods and chattels *plural noun* same as **movable property**

good title *noun* a title to a property that gives the owner full rights of ownership

grade *verb* to level a road or railway

grader *noun* a machine with a wide blade that levels the ground, used in road construction

granny *noun* a revolving cap on a chimney pot

grant *noun* a legal document recording a transaction in which something is transferred from one person to another ■ *verb* to transfer money, property or rights to someone in a legal transaction

grantee *noun* someone who is assigned an interest in a property or who receives a grant

grant of lease *noun* the action of allowing a tenant to occupy a property under the terms of a lease

grantor *noun* a person who assigns an interest in a property, especially to a lender, or who makes a grant

granular loft insulation *noun* a granular substance laid between roof joists to provide insulation

gravity fed system *noun* a domestic water system in which hot water stored in an elevated cylinder flows to the taps by means of gravity, and the hot tank itself is refilled from a cold tank at a higher level

green belt *noun* areas of open countryside on which building is currently not allowed (NOTE: Currently in the UK there is a trend for buying greenbelt land, in the hope that legislation will change and planning permission will be eventually granted.)

green corridor *noun* an area of open countryside between areas of urban development

greenfield *adjective* relating to or situated in a piece of open land that has not been built on

greenhouse *noun* a structure made of glass inside which plants are grown

green mortgage *noun* a mortgage provided by a lender who insists on certain environment-friendly measures being operated in the property

grill *noun* **1.** a device on a cooker that radiates heat downwards **2.** a flat surface of parallel metal bars on which food is grill

grille *noun* a pattern or lattice of bars, especially in front of a window. Also called **grillwork**

grip *noun* a device for holding something firmly

gross income *noun* an individual's income before tax is paid

ground *noun* **1.** an area of land used for a particular purpose **2.** an underlying surface or prepared area that paint is applied to **3.** a first coat of paint applied to a surface being decorated

ground investigation *noun* the use of boring equipment to investigate the structure of ground to be built on

ground landlord *noun* a person or company that owns the freehold of a property that is then leased and subleased

ground lease *noun* the first lease on a freehold building

ground rent *noun* rent paid by a lessee to the ground landlord

ground rent notice *noun* an official notice requiring payment of ground rent

grounds *plural noun* the land surrounding and belonging to a building

ground stabilisation *noun* measures taken to prevent or correct subsidence or slippage of an area of ground

groundworker *noun* 1. a person whose job involves maintaining grounds, especially a junior employee in a local authority's parks and gardens department 2. a builder involved in the first stages of a construction project

grout *noun* 1. thin mortar used to fill gaps, especially between tiles 2. fine plaster used to finish ceilings and walls ■ *verb* to use grout to fill gaps, especially between tiles, or to finish a ceiling or wall

GRP *abbreviation* glass reinforced plastic

guarantee protection insurance *noun* insurance that protects the terms of a contractor's guarantee should the contractor go out of business before the guarantee ends

guarantor *noun* someone who gives a guarantee

guarantor mortgage *noun* a mortgage in which the payments are guaranteed by a third party should the borrower become unable to pay

Guild of Master Craftsmen *noun* a UK trade association representing many different trades and professions and supporting excellence

gully *noun* a gutter, open drain or other artificial channel for water, especially one at a roadside

gusset *noun* a flat, often triangular plate, usually of steel or plywood, used to connect and reinforce a joint where several members meet at different angles, e.g. in a pitched roof

gut *verb* 1. to destroy the internal parts of a building, leaving only the outer walls standing 2. to remove all the internal fixtures and furnishings from a room or building

gutter *noun* 1. a metal or plastic channel fixed to the eaves of a roof for carrying away rainwater 2. a channel at the edge of a road that carries water into a drain

guttering *noun* **1.** the gutters on a roof **2.** metal or plastic channels for use as gutters

gypsum *noun* **1.** a white or colourless mineral, consisting of hydrated calcium, that is an ingredient of plaster and cement **2.** plasterboard (*informal*)

H

habendum *noun* a section of a conveyance that gives details of how the property is to be assigned to the purchaser, using the words 'to hold'

habitable dwelling *noun* a building that is fit to use as a home

habitable room *noun* a room that is fit to live in

habitual residence *noun* **1.** the fact of living normally in a place **2.** the place where someone normally lives

half-landing *noun* a small landing at a mid-point on a staircase, usually where the staircase changes direction

half-timbered *adjective* built with a visible frame of wooden beams as well as plaster, stone, or brick

Halifax House Price Survey *noun* a monthly review of UK house prices carried out by one of the UK's biggest mortgage lenders

hall, hallway *noun* **1.** an entrance room in a house, flat or building, with doors leading to other rooms. Also called **hallway 2.** a connecting passage or corridor with doors leading to other rooms

hammer *noun* a tool with a handle and a heavy metal head, used for knocking in nails or for shaping or breaking surfaces ■ *verb* **1.** to force something such as a nail into something else by pounding it with a hammer **2.** to beat something with a hammer, especially to shape it

hand/arm vibration syndrome *noun* a medical condition caused by frequent use of hand-held vibrating tools such as drills and chainsaws

hand tool *noun* a tool that is powered by hand, not by electricity

hardhat *noun* a helmet made of metal or plastic worn for protection by workers in a factory or on a construction site

hard landscaping *noun* structures such as walls, pavements and fences

hard plaster *noun* plaster used for internal walls, as distinct from plasterboard

hardware *noun* tools and implements, usually made of metal, e.g. hinges, screws and hammers

hardwood *noun* wood from a broad-leaved tree, as distinct from wood from a conifer

hardwood flooring *noun* flooring consisting of hardwood strips or planks, designed to be used uncovered

hatch *noun* **1.** a door cut into a floor or ceiling, lifted to provide access to the area below or above it **2.** a small connecting hole in a wall between two rooms, or the small doors that cover this hole. Also called **hatchway**

hazardous substances *plural noun* chemicals and other substances that can have an adverse effect on health

hazardous waste *noun* a by-product of manufacturing processes that is toxic and can damage people's health or the environment if not treated correctly

header *noun* a brick or stone positioned crosswise in a wall and level with its outer surface. Compare **stretcher**

header tank *noun* a raised tank that ensures a constant pressure or supply of fluid to a system, especially water to a central heating system

headlap *noun* (*in roofing*) the overlap of one course of slates or tiles above the course beneath it

head lease *noun* the first lease given by a freeholder to a tenant

Health and Safety Executive *noun* the executive committee of the Health and Safety Commission. Abbreviation **HSE**

hearth *noun* the floor of a fireplace, especially when it extends into the room

hearthstone *noun* a large stone used to form the hearth in a fireplace

heating *noun* **1.** the operation of warming something such as a room **2.** the equipment that produces heat to warm a room or building, e.g. a central heating system

Heating and Ventilating Contractors' Association *noun* a UK association that represents the interests of firms active in the design, installation, commissioning and maintenance of heating, ventilating, air conditioning and refrigeration equipment

heating engineer *noun* someone trained to install and repair heating systems

heave *noun* unwanted upward movement in the foundations of a building

hedge *noun* a close-set row of bushes, usually with their branches intermingled, forming a barrier or boundary in a garden (NOTE: High hedges are a nuisance listed in the Antisocial Behaviour Act 2003.)

hereditament *noun* property, including land and buildings, that can be inherited

hereditary *adjective* **1.** handed down, or legally capable of being handed down, through generations by inheritance **2.** holding a right, function or property by right of inheritance

heritable property *noun* (*in Scotland*) property in the form of land and houses

heritage *noun* (*in Scotland*) property or land that is or can be passed on to an heir

High Court, High Court of Justice *noun* the main civil court in England and Wales

High Court of Justiciary *noun* the supreme criminal court of Scotland

higher lending charge *noun* a fee charged by a mortgage lender when the amount borrowed exceeds a given percentage of the value of the property

high income multiplier mortgage *noun* a mortgage in which the loan amount exceeds the normal 2 or 3 times the borrower's main income

high lending fee, high loan-to-value fee *noun* a fee that a borrower may be charged if he or she applies to borrow more than 90% or 95% of the property's value

high-pitched *adjective* having a very steep slope

high-rise *noun* a multistorey building, especially a block of flats

high-voltage power line *noun* a cable that carries high-voltage electricity, usually buried underground or carried high above ground on pylons

highway *noun* any public road (*formal*)

Highways Agency *noun* an executive agency of the UK Department for Transport responsible for operating, maintaining and improving the strategic road network in England

hinge *noun* a movable joint of metal or plastic used to fasten together two things, e.g. a box and its lid, and allow one of them to pivot

Hire Association Europe *noun* the leading trade association for hire and rental companies in the UK and Ireland

Historic Scotland *noun* an agency within the Scottish Executive Education Department responsible for safeguarding the nation's historic environment and promoting its understanding and enjoyment

HMO *abbreviation* Home in Multiple Occupation

HM Revenue and Customs *noun* a UK government department responsible for collecting taxes and duties

hoarding *noun* a tall fence used to screen off a building site

hod *noun* a V-shaped tray on the end of a long pole, usually carried on the shoulder, used for carrying bricks, mortar and other building materials

hoist *noun* a mechanical device or apparatus designed for lifting heavy objects

holder *noun* someone who owns, occupies or is in possession of something such as property or a title

holding *noun* a piece of land that is leased from someone else, especially when used for agricultural purposes

holdover tenancy *noun* a situation in which a tenant continues to occupy a property after the lease has expired, against the wishes of the landlord, but continues to fulfil the terms of the tenancy

holiday home *noun* a house in which a person only lives for part of the time, such as at weekends or during a holiday. Also called **second home** (NOTE: If a holiday home is rented out as a business for more than 140 days a year, business rates become payable.)

home *noun* **1.** the place where a person, family or household lives **2.** a family or any other group that lives together

HomeBuy agent *noun* a housing association that operates as a point of contact for people seeking affordable housing in a particular area

homebuyer's report *noun* a survey that is less comprehensive than a full structural survey but gives a good indication of the state of the property and its level of repair and maintenance

HomeBuy scheme *noun* a UK government initiative designed to enable key workers and other first time buyers to buy a share of a home and get a first step on the property ladder

home condition report *noun* a survey on the condition of the property that can be relied upon by buyers, sellers and mortgage lenders

home information pack *noun* a set of documents giving comprehensive information on many aspects of a property being bought or sold, e.g. various searches conducted, copies of the deeds and information regarding energy efficiency, provided in accordance with a UK government scheme introduced in June 2007

Home in Multiple Occupation *noun* a property which is subdivided into two or more separate living quarters. Abbreviation **HMO**

home inspector *noun* a trained professional who prepares documents for a home information pack

Homelink *noun* an international organisation that arranges home exchanges and house swaps

home makeover *noun* a process in which the interior decoration of a home is completely refurbished and restyled

home makeover show *noun* a television programme that features home makeovers and improvements

home renovation grant *noun* a grant provided by a local authority to help owners of properties in poor condition carry out repairs to bring their homes up to a recognised standard

home reversion plan, home reversion scheme *noun* a scheme that is similar to an equity release plan but that involves the homeowner selling all or some of the property to the plan provider

home stager *noun* an agent who gives advice on how to make a home for sale appealing to potential buyers

home staging *noun* the work of a home stager

Homestake *noun* (*in Scotland*) a scheme aimed at helping people on low incomes who want to own their own homes but who cannot afford to pay the full price

Homeswap *noun* a UK-wide register of Council, Housing Association and Housing Co-operative tenants who want to swap homes

Hometrack *noun* an index designed to give up-to-date and accurate information about UK house prices and trends down to postcode level

hood *noun* a fixed or revolving cover fitted to the top of a chimney to prevent downdraught

hot water cylinder *noun* a cylindrical tank in which domestic hot water is heated, usually by means of an electrical element immersed in the water. Also called **immersion tank**

House Builders Federation *noun* the principal UK trade organisation for private sector housebuilders

household waste recovery centre *noun* a centre where recyclable material is sorted, crushed and baled before being sold for reprocessing

house hunt *noun* a search for a residential property to buy or rent

house hunter *noun* someone looking to buy or rent a house

house in multiple occupation *noun* a residential property that was originally built for a single household but is now occupied by two or more households who share common areas such as a kitchen or stairwell

house inspection *noun* a general term for a survey

house price survey *noun US* a survey

house price to earnings ratio *noun* an economic indicator calculated by dividing the average house price in an area by the average income

house sit *verb* to live in temporarily and take care of someone else's house and property while that person is away

housing *noun* 1. houses and other buildings where people live, considered collectively 2. the provision of places to live 3. a slot, groove or hole in one piece of wood into which another piece is fitted

Housing (Scotland) Act 1988 *noun* a piece of UK legislation that set out local authority duties to provide housing for certain groups of homeless people in Scotland

Housing Act 2004 *noun* a piece of UK legislation that brings in several reforms to protect tenants, bring empty homes back into use and tackle antisocial behaviour in relation to property

Housing Acts *plural noun* the various pieces of UK legislation that relate to domestic property

housing association *noun* a non-profit making organisation that provides houses and flats at fair rents

Housing Association Property Mutual scheme *noun* a scheme that assists housing association tenants who wish to swap homes

housing benefit *noun* a local government benefit paid to people who cannot pay their rent

Housing Corporation *noun* the government agency that funds new affordable housing and regulates housing associations in England and Wales

housing department *noun* the department of a local authority responsible for housing in its area

housing market *noun* the sale of houses. Also called **property market**

Housing Ombudsman Service *noun* an independent service dealing with complaints against landlords and agents and with other housing disputes

housing stock *noun* the number of habitable houses in an area

HSE *abbreviation* Health and Safety Executive

HVAC *abbreviation* heating, ventilation and air conditioning

hydraulic excavator *noun* a vehicle with a large hydraulic digging and earth-moving arm, usually running on tracks

hypothec *noun* (*in Scotland*) a creditor's right to have his or her debt paid from the proceeds of the sale of a debtor's property, or to become the owner of the property if the debtor defaults on the debt

hypothecate *verb* to pledge property or goods as security for a debt without surrendering ownership

hypothecation *noun* **1.** the use of property such as securities as collateral for a loan, without transferring legal ownership to the lender, which is not the case with a mortgage, where the lender holds the title to the property **2.** the action of earmarking money derived from specific sources for related expenditure, e.g. investing the taxes from private cars or petrol sales solely in public transport

I

I-beam *noun* a metal beam or girder that is shaped like a capital 'I' in cross section

IBI *abbreviation* impuesto sobre bienes inmuebles

ichnography *noun* 1. the art or practice of drawing ground plans of the layout of buildings 2. a ground plan of the layout of a building

ICI *abbreviation* imposta comunale sugli immobili

identity check *noun* a check carried out to verify the identity of a potential buyer or seller of property

IFA *abbreviation* independent financial advisor

IHT *abbreviation* Institution of Highways and Transportation

illumination *noun* the amount or strength of light available in a place or for a purpose

illustration *noun* a drawing, picture, photograph or diagram that accompanies and complements a text

immersion tank *noun* same as **hot water cylinder**

immovable property *noun* houses and other buildings on land, as well as land itself

implied term *noun* a term in a contract that is not clearly set out in the contract. Compare **express term**

implied trust *noun* a trust that is implied by the intentions and actions of the parties

imposta comunale sugli immobili *noun* (*in Italy*) the equivalent of council tax. Abbreviation **ICI**

imposta sul valore aggiunto *noun* (*in Italy*) the equivalent of VAT. Abbreviation **IVA**

imposto de selo *noun* (*in Portugal*) stamp duty

imposto municipal sobre as transmissões *noun* (*in Portugal*) a municipal property transfer tax. Abbreviation **IMT**

imposto sobre as sucessões e doações *noun* (*in Portugal*) inheritance tax

imposto sobre o valor acrescentado *noun* (*in Portugal*) value-added tax

impôt de solidarité sur la fortune *noun* (*in France*) wealth tax, charged on all high-value assets including land and buildings

improve *verb* to make property such as land or buildings more valuable

improvement *noun* **1.** a change or addition to property or land that increases value **2.** an increase in the value of property or land

improvement grant *noun* a grant available to improve the standard of a building or an area (NOTE: Grants are available for a variety of purposes, for example the installation of domestic drainage and bathrooms, the eradication of bracken on pasture land or the provision of a water supply for agricultural land.)

impuesto de plusvalía *noun* (*in Spain*) a local capital gains tax

impuesto sobre bienes inmuebles *noun* (*in Spain*) residential property tax, a local tax charged on all residential properties that are used, or are available for use, by the owner

impuesto sobre el valor añadido *noun* (*in Spain*) the equivalent of VAT. Abbreviation **IVA**

impuesto sobre la renta de no residentes *noun* (*in Spain*) an income tax on rental property

IMT *abbreviation* imposto municipal sobre as transmissões

incendiary *adjective* **1.** able to catch fire spontaneously or cause a fire easily **2.** relating to or involving the illegal burning of property

included in sale *adjective* used for referring to all items in, or relating to, a property that are included in the sale price

income *noun* the amount of money received over a period of time either as payment for work, goods, or services, or as profit on capital (NOTE: Income is used when calculating mortgage lending limits.)

income from property *noun* income from sources connected with the ownership of property, e.g. the rental payments of tenants

income multiple *noun* a homebuyer's loan the value of which is calculated in multiples of the applicant's income, as most loans are

income protection *noun* insurance that provides the policyholder with a monthly income if he or she is unable to work owing to sickness or accidental injury, to help maintain a standard of living

income reference *noun* the year to which information about income refers

incorporeal hereditaments *plural noun* rights such as patents or copyrights that can form part of an estate and be inherited

incremento de valor de bienes de naturaleza urbana *noun* (*in Spain*) a local capital gains tax

incumbrance *noun* same as **encumbrance**

indemnité d'immobilisation *noun* (*in France*) a deposit on a home, usually between 5% and 10% of the property purchase price

indemnity covenant *noun* a clause in a transfer document in which the buyer undertakes to compensate the seller if the buyer breaches in any of the restrictions in the title deeds that affect the property

indemnity insurance *noun* insurance cover that protects a professional against claims for damages that clients make against him or her

independent financial advisor *noun* a professional who offers financial advice on a full range of products from all companies on the market and whose fees are paid by the client directly, not by the company whose products he or she sells or recommends

Independent Housing Ombudsman *noun* an official who investigates complaints about the actions or omissions of private landlords by their tenants and others who receive a direct service from them

independent qualified conveyancer *noun* a professional person who is not a solicitor but is licensed to carry out conveyancing work

Independent Surveyors Association *noun* an association of independent surveying and valuation practices offering independent advice to property buyers and lenders

index-linked insurance *noun* insurance in which the premiums increase each year in line with inflation to account for the declining real value of the policy

index map search *noun* a Land Registry service that identifies a property and identifies any registrations and applications currently being registered that affect it

index tracker mortgage *noun* a type of mortgage in which the rate of interest charged follows exactly any changes in a particular interest rate, e.g. the Bank of England base rate

individual mortgage *noun* a mortgage in which the borrower is a single private individual

Individual Savings Account *noun* full form of **ISA**

industrial estate *noun* an area of land near a town specially for factories and warehouses

infestation *noun* the presence of large numbers of pests

infill development *noun* the development of parcels of land that were not developed when the rest of the area was originally developed

inflation rate *noun* a figure, in the form of a percentage, that shows the amount by which inflation has increased over a period of time, usually a year. Also called **rate of inflation**

infra-red camera *noun* a piece of equipment used in mechanical and electrical surveys to detect a range of temperature-related faults

infringement *noun* an act of breaking a law or not respecting a right

infringement of building regulations *noun* a situation in which someone has breached building regulations

inglenook *noun* **1.** a recess for a seat or bench beside a large fireplace, sometimes covered by the chimney-breast **2.** a seat built in an inglenook, especially one of two benches or chairs facing each other

inheritance *noun* property that is received by someone from a person who has died

inheritance tax *noun* a tax levied on property received by inheritance or legal succession, calculated according to the value of the property received

injunction *noun* **1.** a court order that requires someone involved in a legal action to do something or refrain from doing something **2.** a command or order, especially from someone in a position of authority

injurious falsehood *noun* the offence of making a wrong statement about someone so as to harm their reputation, usually in relation to their business or property

Inland Revenue *noun* in the United Kingdom, a government body responsible for the collection and administration of direct taxes such as income tax and corporation tax

in possession *adverb* in a position to enjoy now any rights or benefits relating to a property

insolvency *noun* the state of not being able to pay debts

insolvent *adjective* **1.** unable to pay debts **2.** relating to people or businesses that are bankrupt

inspection *noun* a thorough examination of something with the aim of forming an opinion or making a judgement

installation *noun* **1.** the process of putting a piece of equipment or machinery in place and making it ready for use **2.** a system or piece of equipment that has been put in place and made ready for use

Institute of Building Control *noun* a UK body that concerns itself exclusively with building control, offering a widely recognised qualification supported by training and educational courses

Institute of Carpenters *noun* a UK institute that administers qualifications in carpentry and also has links with training boards, technical research bodies and the trading standards authorities

Institute of Highway Incorporated Engineers *noun* the professional body for incorporated engineers and technicians in all aspects of construction, highway and traffic engineering and transport

Institute of Plumbing *noun* a UK registered educational charity with the aim of improving the science and practice of plumbing and heating engineering

Institution of Civil Engineers *noun* a UK institution that is a qualifying body, a centre for the exchange of specialist knowledge, and a provider of resources to encourage innovation and excellence in the civil engineering profession

Institution of Engineering and Technology *noun* a global information service for all professionals engaged in engineering and technology

Institution of Highways and Transportation *noun* a UK institution that aims to promote the exchange of knowledge, improve policy formulation and stimulate debate on transportation issues. Abbreviation **IHT**

Institution of Structural Engineers *noun* an international professional body for structural engineering that qualifies its members by examinations that test professional competence

insulate *verb* to prevent or reduce the passage of heat, electricity or sound into, from or through something, especially by surrounding it with some material

insulating glass *noun* glass that is a combination of two or more panes enclosing a hermetically sealed air space, designed to reduce heat loss from buildings

insulation *noun* **1.** material that prevents or reduces the passage of heat, electricity or sound, e.g. a special fabric or a layer of air **2.** the act of covering or surrounding something to prevent or reduce the passage of heat, electricity or sound

insulation tape *noun* plastic-coated tape used for electrical work

insurance *noun* **1.** an arrangement by which a company gives customers financial protection against loss or harm such as theft of or damage to property, in return for payment **2.** the sum of money that an insurance company pays or agrees to pay if a specific undesirable event occurs **3.** the payment made to obtain insurance

insurance cover *noun* protection guaranteed by an insurance policy

insurance policy *noun* a document that shows the conditions of an insurance contract

insurance premium *noun* a payment made by the insured person to an insurance company

insurer *noun* a company that insures someone or something

intangible assets *plural noun* business assets, e.g. a customer's goodwill, that are of value although they are not directly quantifiable in terms of goods produced or sold. Compare **tangible assets**

intercommunicate *verb* to be connected to another room by means of a door in the dividing wall

interest *noun* **1.** a payment made by a borrower for the use of money, calculated as a percentage of the capital borrowed **2.** money paid as income on investments or loans **3.** a percentage charge to be paid for borrowing money **4.** the right or title to a property

interest in remainder *noun* an interest in land that will come into someone's possession when another person's interest ends

interest-only mortgage *noun* a mortgage in which the monthly payments pay only the interest on the loan, with the outstanding balance usually paid at the end of the loan from the proceeds of an endowment policy

interest rate *noun* a percentage charge to be paid for borrowing money

interior *noun* the inside of a building or room considered especially with regard to its decoration and furnishing

interior decoration *noun* **1.** the way that a room or building is decorated and furnished **2.** the skill or trade of someone who specialises in wallpapering and painting interiors

interior designer *noun* a professional who gives advice on interior decoration

interior outfitting *noun* same as **interior decoration**

internal *adjective* situated on the inside of a building

internal door *noun* a door that connects two internal rooms in a building, as distinct from a door that leads to outside

internal wall structure *noun* the method of constructing an interior wall, e.g. the use of hard plaster or the use of a timber frame and plasterboard

international mortgage *noun* a mortgage for an overseas property, or a mortgage for a domestic property in which overseas funds are used

inventory *noun* a complete list of all the things included in something such as a house for sale or rent, or the estate of a deceased person ■ *verb* to make a list of the contents of a property

investigation of title *noun* a check into the precise nature of the title to a property

investment home loan *noun* same as **buy to let mortgage**

investment property *noun* a property that is bought and held for the purpose of letting

investor *noun* a person, company or other organisation that has money invested in something

inward investment *noun* an investment from outside a country, as when a foreign company decides to set up a new factory there

ironmongery *noun* items such as door hinges and window catches, made of metal

irrigation system *noun* a system that delivers water to an area of land, usually agricultural or horticultural land

irritancy *noun* (*in Scotland*) the forfeiture of a right through failure to abide by the law or an agreement, as occurs, e.g., when a tenant fails to pay rent due

ISA *noun* a British scheme by which individuals can invest for their retirement by putting a limited amount of money each year in a tax-free account. Full form **Individual Savings Account**

ISA mortgage *noun* a mortgage in which an individual savings account is paid into, to build up a capital lump sum, and the capital is used at the end of the mortgage term to pay off the loan, running alongside an interest-only mortgage

Islamic finance *noun* finance provided by Islamic financial institutions, many of which conduct their business according to Sharia or traditional Islamic law

Islamic mortgage *noun* a mortgage that complies with the Sharia prohibition on paying or receiving interest. Also called **Sharia-compliant mortgage**

issue *noun* a legal matter in a dispute between two parties

IVA *abbreviation* **1.** imposta sul valore aggiunto **2.** imposto sobre o valore acrescentado **3.** impuesto sobre el valor añadido

J

jamb *noun* **1.** either of the upright parts of a door or window frame or the sides of a fireplace **2.** the inside vertical face of an opening

jawbreaker *noun* a machine that crushes rocks using powerful jaws

joggle *noun* a joint between two pieces of masonry or concrete, in which a projection on one fits into a recess of the other ■ *verb* to join pieces of masonry or concrete with a joggle

joiner *noun* someone who makes wooden components for buildings, especially finished woodwork

joinery *noun* **1.** the visible finished woodwork in a building, e.g. door frames and window frames **2.** the work of a joiner, or the techniques that a joiner uses

joint *adjective* owned in common by two or more people or concerns ■ *noun* a place or building (*slang*)

joint agency *noun* a situation in which a seller appoints two agents to sell a property, in which commission is often higher as each claims to have only half the chance of earning it

joint and several liability *noun* a situation in which two or more parties share a single liability, and each party is also liable for the whole claim

jointer *noun* **1.** a tool for pointing the mortar in brickwork or stonework after it has been laid **2.** a long plane used to shape the edges of planks into joints

joint income *noun* the combined income of two or more individuals making a joint application for a mortgage

joint liability *noun* a situation in which two or more parties share a single liability

joint ownership *noun* a situation in which two or more persons own the same property

joint tenancy *noun* a situation in which two or more persons acquire an interest in a property together, and, if one of the joint tenants dies, his or her share goes to those surviving. ◊ **tenancy in common**

joint tenants *plural noun* ownership by two or more tenants that gives each an equal share of a piece of property

judicial review *noun* a reassessment or re-examination by judges of a decision or proceeding by a lower court or a government department

Juliet balcony *noun* a balcony that simply affords a view from an upstairs French window and has no surface for standing or sitting on

jus accrescendi *noun* the fact that, on the death of a joint tenant, his or her rights and ownership pass to the surviving joint tenants and cannot be transferred under the terms of a will

K

kerb *noun* a raised edge of stone or concrete separating the pavement from the road or street

kerb brace *noun* a reinforcing piece at a joint between two high kerbstones

kerb lifter *noun* any of various machines for lowering kerbstones into place

kerbside collection *noun* a system of collecting domestic refuse in which residents place bins at the kerbside

kerbstone *noun* any of the large stones used to make a kerb

key *noun* **1.** a metal bar with notches or grooves that, when inserted into a lock and turned, operates the lock's mechanism **2.** the process of preparing a surface, usually by making it rough or grooved, so that paint or some other finish will stick to it **3.** same as **keystone** ■ *verb* **1.** to prepare a surface, usually by making it rough or grooved, so that paint or another finish will stick to it **2.** to provide an arch with a keystone

keyfacts illustration *trademark* a tradename for a document provided by a mortgage lender that summarises the important features of the mortgage (NOTE: The document must be clear, fair and not misleading and will be presented in a standard way, so a customer can easily check the cost and terms of the mortgage and compare it with other similar mortgages.)

key money *noun* a premium paid when taking over the keys of a flat or office being rented

keystone *noun* the wedge-shaped stone at the highest point of an arch that locks the others in place

key worker *noun* someone who works in a public service, e.g. teaching, nursing or the prison service

key worker living programme *noun* a programme designed to provide affordable housing for key workers

key worker loan *noun* a government loan that allows a key worker on low income to pay a deposit on a property

kilowatt *noun* a unit of measurement of electricity equal to 1000 watts. Symbol **kW**

kilowatt hour *noun* a unit of energy equal to the work done by one kilowatt in one hour. Symbol **kWh**

kitchen *noun* a room or part of a room or building in which food is prepared and cooked

kitchen diner *noun* a kitchen that is large enough to include an area for dining, usually a fairly small area

kitchen fitments *plural noun* non-moveable items such as cupboards that are built into a kitchen

knacker *noun* someone who buys and demolishes unwanted buildings and sells their materials for scrap

L

labour *noun* physical work done by labourers

labourer *noun* someone who does unskilled work

lagging *noun* **1.** insulating material used to keep heat from escaping, especially round a pipe or hot water tank **2.** a wooden frame used in building, especially to support an arch while it is being built

lamella *noun* a structural part of wood, metal or reinforced concrete that is crisscrossed to form a vault

laminate *verb* **1.** to cover something with a thin sheet of protective material such as plastic or metal **2.** to bond sheets or layers together so as to produce a strong and durable composite material ■ *noun* a product composed of layers or sheets bonded together

laminate floor *noun* flooring in the form of strips or boards of a wooden composite material with a solid wood veneer

lamp holder *noun* the part of a light or lamp into which the bulb fits directly

land agent *noun* someone who manages a farm or large area of land for someone else

land certificate *noun* a document that shows who owns a piece of land and whether there are any charges on it

land charges *plural noun* covenants, mortgages or other charges attached to a piece of land

land charges register *noun* a register of matters affecting a property or piece of land, e.g. whether road building is planned nearby or whether a public footpath crosses it, kept by a local authority

land charges search *noun* a check for any matters affecting a property or piece of land, usually requested by a solicitor or licensed conveyancer on behalf of a potential buyer

land compensation *noun* compensation that can be obtained if intolerable noise cannot be reduced and its presence reduces the value of surrounding property

landfill *noun* **1.** same as **landfill site 2.** the disposal of waste material or refuse by burying it in natural or excavated holes or depressions

landfill site *noun* an area of land where waste is put into holes in the ground and covered with earth. Also called **landfill**

landing *noun* a platform between flights of stairs, or the floor at the top or foot of a flight of stairs

landlady *noun* a woman who owns a property that she lets

landline *noun* a telephone that is not a mobile phone or satellite phone

landlord *noun* a person or company that owns a property that is let

Landlord and Tenant Act *noun* a piece of UK legislation that regulates the letting of property

landlord registration *noun* (*in Scotland*) the fact that all private landlords are required to register with their local authority who supervises standards and takes action against irresponsible landlords

landlord's reference *noun* a reference from previous landlords, supplied by someone seeking to rent accommodation from a new landlord

landowner *noun* someone who owns large areas of land

land raising *noun* the use of land for the purposes of waste disposal

Land Reform (Scotland) Act 2003 *noun* a piece of legislation that establishes statutory rights of access to land and inland water in Scotland for outdoor recreation

land register *noun* an official register of land in England and Wales, compiled by a Government department, showing who owns it and what buildings are on it

Land Registers Scotland *noun* the official register of land and property in Scotland

land registrar *noun* an official who heads one of the 24 local offices of the Land Register

land registration *noun* a system of registering land and its owners

Land Registration Act 1925 *noun* the legislation that was replaced in its entirety by the Land Registration Act 2002

Land Registration Act 2002 *noun* a piece of UK legislation introduced with the aim of making the official register of land as comprehensive as possible, partly in order to facilitate e-conveyancing

Land Registry *noun* the UK government office where details of land and its ownership are kept

Land Registry Residential Property Price Report *noun* a quarterly report that provides information on average house prices for numerous categories of housing

land required for public purposes *noun* land for which planning permission will only be granted by a local authority for building work that serves a public purpose

lands *plural noun* large areas of land owned by one owner

landscaped *adjective* with the natural features of land modified for aesthetic purposes, e.g. by grading ground, or planting trees and shrubs

landscape gardener *noun* a designer of grounds and gardens

landscaping *noun* **1.** the enhancement of the appearance of land, especially around buildings, by altering its contours and planting trees, shrubs and flowers **2.** the profession of designing or creating gardens by combining plants and other features to produce a pleasing overall effect

Lands Tribunal *noun* a court that deals with compensation claims relating to land (NOTE: The Lands Tribunal deals with disputes over easements, restrictive covenants, land valuations and compensation for compulsory purchases, and hears appeals from the residential property and leasehold valuation tribunals.)

Lands Tribunal for Scotland *noun* (*in Scotland*) an independent civil court with the statutory power to deal with various types of dispute involving land or property

land surveyor *noun* a professional who measures and charts the precise shape of natural and artificial features on a site's surface. This data forms the basis of plans used for civil engineering and construction projects.

land tax *noun* a tax on the amount of land owned

land tenure *noun* a way in which land is owned, e.g. leasehold or freehold

land to be acquired for road works *noun* land on which a public authority will at some point be building a road

lapse *noun* a failure to exercise a right within a specific period of time, e.g. failure to buy a property before the termination of an option to buy ∎ *verb* to become null and void through disuse, negligence, or death

last time buyer *noun* a mature person who is unlikely to be moving house after the current property is purchased

late charge *noun* a penalty for failing to pay a mortgage instalment on time

late completion *noun* a situation in which the seller of property fails to complete the contract at the agreed time (NOTE: Late completion usually incurs a penalty, as the delay can cause financial loss and associated problems for the other party and those in the chain.)

late payment *noun* a failure to pay a mortgage instalment on time

lateral restraint *noun* the mutual structural support that is created when floor or roof members are properly fixed to the walls of a building

lath *noun* **1.** one of the thin strips of wood used to form a framework to support plaster, tiles or slates **2.** a sheet of metal or a framework of wire mesh used as a support for plasterwork ∎ *verb* to nail laths to a surface before plastering, tiling or fixing slates

lattice *noun* **1.** an interwoven open-mesh frame made by crisscrossing strips of wood, metal or plastic to form a pattern. Also called **latticework 2.** something, e.g. a door, gate, or fence, that is made from or consists of a lattice

laundry *noun* a place, especially a commercial establishment or a communal room in a building, where clothes and linen can be washed and ironed

lavatory *noun* a toilet, or a small room containing a toilet

Law Commission *noun* a permanent committee that reviews English law and recommends changes to it

lawful development certificate *noun* a statutory document, issued by a local authority planning department, confirming that the use, operation or activity named in it is lawful for planning control purposes

law of property *noun* a branch of the law dealing with the rights of ownership

Law of Property Act 1925 *noun* a piece of UK legislation substantially amended by the Law of Property (Miscellaneous Provisions) Act 1989

Law of Property (Miscellaneous Provisions) Act 1989 *noun* a piece of UK legislation that, among other things, makes it necessary that agreements for the disposition of interests in land are in writing

law of succession *noun* law relating to how property shall pass to others when the owner dies

Law Society *noun* an organisation of solicitors in England and Wales, which represents and regulates the profession

Law Society (Northern Ireland) *noun* a professional organisation that regulates the solicitors' profession in Northern Ireland

Law Society (Scotland) *noun* a professional organisation that regulates the solicitors' profession in Scotland

LCHO *abbreviation* low-cost home ownership

leaf *noun* **1.** a hinged or removable section of a table top **2.** a hinged or sliding section of a door, shutter or gate

lean-to *noun* an outbuilding with a slanted roof that rests against the wall of a larger building

lease *noun* a written contract for the renting of a building or piece of land (NOTE: There are different types of lease, and they may be discussed and amended before signing.) ■ *verb* **1.** to let or rent a building or piece of land **2.** to use a building or piece of land in return for paying a fee to the landlord

lease back *verb* to sell a property to someone and then retake possession of it on a lease

lease-back *noun* an arrangement by which property is sold and then taken back on a lease

lease extension *noun* an agreement to extend a lease beyond the term originally agreed on (NOTE: Under the Commonhold and Leasehold Reform Act 2002, leaseholders have the automatic right to extend their lease after owning a property for 2 years.)

leasehold *noun* a property that is held for a period of time on the basis of a lease

leasehold absolute *noun* the most secure form of title to leasehold land, in which the owner is vested with all rights and privileges attached to the land

Leasehold Advisory Service *noun* a UK organisation that provides free advice on the law affecting residential long leasehold property and commonhold

leasehold agreement *noun* a legal document that establishes a leasehold

leasehold enfranchisement *noun* the right of a leaseholder to buy the freehold of the property that he or she is leasing

Leasehold Enfranchisement Advisory Service *noun* a UK organisation that provides advice to leaseholders on the purchase of his or her freehold or on the extension of his or her lease

leaseholder *noun* someone who holds a property on a lease

leaseholder enfranchisement rights *noun* the right of a leaseholder to buy the freehold on his or her property or to extend the term of the lease

leaseholder's obligations *plural noun* obligations such as the payment of any ground rent and a contribution to the costs of maintaining and managing the building

leasehold possessory *noun* a leasehold title given in cases where the applicant's title cannot be proved because the deeds have been lost or destroyed

leasehold property *noun* a property held under a leasehold

leasehold qualified *noun* a leasehold title given where the land registrar considers that the applicant's title can only be established for a limited period

leasehold valuation tribunal *noun* a tribunal established to settle disputes between freeholders and leaseholders

legacy *noun* money or property that is left to someone in a will

legal charge *noun* a charge created over property by a legal mortgage

legal claim *noun* a statement that someone owns something legally

legal fee *noun* a fee charged by a lawyer or conveyancer for legal services

legal proceedings *plural noun* a case that is brought to court or to a tribunal

Legal Services Ombudsman *noun* an official who examines whether a complaint made against a lawyer was adequately dealt with by the lawyer's own professional body

legal title *noun* the right to be regarded as the legal owner of property

legislature *noun* the part of a government that makes or changes laws (NOTE: The other parts are the **executive** and the **judiciary**.)

lender *noun* someone who lends money

lessee *noun* a person who pays rent for a property he or she leases from a lessor

lessor *noun* someone who grants a lease on a property to a lessee

let *verb* **1.** to allow someone to do something **2.** to lend a property to someone in return for payment ■ *noun* a period of the lease of a property

let out *verb* to make a place available for letting

letting agency *noun* an agency that deals in property to let

letting agent *noun* an agent who arranges for property to be let

lettings management *noun* the business of managing the letting of property

lettings relief *noun* tax relief granted on income from let property

level *noun* **1.** (*in surveying*) an instrument used to measure the relative heights of different points in the landscape **2.** (*in surveying*) a measurement taken of the relative heights of different points in a landscape **3.** *US* same as **spirit level** ■ *verb* (*in surveying*) to measure the elevation of an area of land

lever mortice deadlock *noun* a mortice deadlock with a lever action, as distinct from a cylinder action

levy *verb* to seize property in accordance with a legal ruling

liability *noun* legal responsibility for something, especially costs or damages

LIBOR *abbreviation* London Inter-Bank Offered Rate

LIBOR-linked mortgage *noun* a mortgage in which the rate of interest is linked to the London Inter-Bank Offered Rate

library *noun* a room, building or institution where a collection of books or other research materials is kept

licença de habitação *noun* (*in Portugal*) a licence that shows that a property is compliant with appropriate building regulations

licence *noun* **1.** a printed document that gives official permission to a specific person or group to own something or do something **2.** official permission to do something, either from a government or under a law or regulation

licence to assign *noun* a document that a landlord signs to allow a tenant to sell the lease to the property

licencia de obra *noun* (*in Spain*) a building licence, usually required if renovation work to a property involves changes to the outside of the property

licencia de primera ocupación *noun* (*in Spain*) a licence of first occupation, one of several licences required when a property has been built

licensed conveyancer *noun* someone who is qualified to carry out conveyancing work but is not a qualified solicitor

licensed conveyancing *noun* the work of a licensed conveyancer

licensee *noun* a person who has a licence allowing them to carry out an activity such as manufacturing or extracting something

licensor *noun* a person who licenses someone

lien *noun* the legal right to keep or sell someone else's property as security for a debt

life assurance *noun* insurance that pays a sum of money when someone dies, or at a specified date if the person is still alive

life assured *adjective* the person whose life is insured against death under the terms of a policy

life insurance *noun* same as **life assurance**

life interest *noun* a situation in which someone benefits from a property as long as he or she is alive

liferent *noun* (*in Scotland*) the right to use and enjoy another's property for the duration of a lifetime

lifetime mortgage *noun* a loan for mature borrowers, secured against property and repaid after death from the proceeds of the sale of the property

light *noun* **1.** an artificial source of illumination, e.g. an electric lamp or a candle **2.** a window or other opening in a building, designed to let sunlight in

lightbulb *noun* a near-spherical glass case containing a filament that emits light when an electric current is passed through it

light well *noun* an area of a building into which a lot of natural light enters, usually from above

lime *verb* **1.** to cover a surface with whitewash **2.** to treat wood with calcium carbonate to give it a pale bleached appearance

limestone mining search *noun* a check, conducted on behalf of a prospective housebuyer, for evidence of limestone mining in the area of the house, which may lead to concerns over subsidence

limitation *noun* a legal restriction on the powers that someone has

limitation of actions *noun* a law that allows only a specific amount of time, usually six years, for someone to start legal proceedings in order to claim property or compensation for damage

limited title guarantee *noun* a title given by a seller in a situation in which, because of his or her limited knowledge of the property, the full title guarantee cannot be given

line and pins *noun* a bricklayer's tool consisting of a line attached to two pins, used for marking a level line for laying to

linen cupboard *noun* a large cupboard in a house for storing linen, towels and similar items

lining paper *noun* paper applied to a wall, usually horizontally, before the decorative paper is pasted

link detached *adjective* used for describing a property that is attached to a neighbouring property via the garage

lintel *noun* a horizontal beam that supports the weight of the wall above a door or window

liquidate *verb* **1.** to wind up a business, paying off its liabilities from its assets, or cease trading as a business in this way **2.** to turn assets into cash

liquidator *noun* someone who administers the assets and supervises the winding up of a company

list *verb* to state officially that a building is one of a group that cannot be demolished or altered without government permission because they are of special architectural or historical importance

listed building *noun* a building of special architectural or historical importance that the owners cannot demolish or significantly alter without planning permission

listed building consent *noun* consent required in order to carry out any works to a listed building that will affect its special value for listing purposes

listed building enforcement notice *noun* an official notice establishing the status of a listed building and setting out the restrictions on building work that must be complied with

listed building purchase notice *noun* a notice that requires a local authority to purchase a listed building in cases where the restrictions deriving from listed building status make the building incapable of beneficial use

litigant *noun* someone who brings a lawsuit against someone else

litigation *noun* the act or process of bringing or contesting a lawsuit

load-bearing wall *noun* an interior wall that supports some weight. Also called **bearing wall**

loader *noun* a machine used for loading heavy construction materials and transporting them

loam *noun* **1.** an easily worked fertile soil consisting of a mixture of clay, sand and silt and sometimes also organic matter **2.** a mixture of moist clay and sand used for making bricks and in plastering

loan *noun* an amount of money given to somebody on the condition that it will be paid back later ■ *verb* to allow someone to borrow something, especially money, on the condition that it is returned

loan consolidation *noun* the practice of paying off several separate debts by means of a single loan, theoretically making the debt more manageable

loan-to-value *adjective* used for expressing the relationship between the amount of a mortgage and the value of the property on which it is taken out. Abbreviation **LTV**

lobby *noun* a large entrance hall or foyer immediately inside the door of a hotel, theatre or other public building

local authority *noun* an elected section of government that runs a small area of the country (NOTE: Local Authorities undertake local searches in property transactions and oversee council tax payment, housing benefits and building control.)

local authority search *noun* a check, carried out by a solicitor or conveyancer as part of the conveyancing process, of any plans that might affect the property a client is considering buying

local development document *noun* a document, provided by a local authority planning department, that sets out their strategy for the development and use of land in their area of authority

local development framework *noun* a portfolio of local development documents

local development order *noun* a later addition made to a local development document which modifies it

local development scheme *noun* a public statement of a local authority's programme for the preparation of local development documents

Local Government Ombudsman *noun* an official who investigates complaints about most council matters, including housing, planning, education and social services

Local Land Charges Act 1975 *noun* a piece of UK legislation that places a duty on local authorities to keep an up-to-date register of charges affecting land and property

Local Nature Reserve *noun* a local-authority area designated as important for its nature and on which development is therefore restricted

local search *noun* a check of a local land charges register for any legal obligations enforceable against the property by the local authority, e.g. financial charges or planning and highway issues

Local Strategic Partnership *noun* a body that seeks to bring together at a local level the different parts of the public, private, community and voluntary sectors

location *noun* the site or position of something

location, location, location *noun* an emphatic expression of the view that a property's location is its most important asset

locator *noun* a device which is used to locate hidden cables or pipes in a building

lock-in clause *noun* an agreement between a seller and an estate agent that specifies how much time the agent has to sell a property before another agent is instructed

lock-in period *noun* a period during which a restriction relating to the purchase or sale of property is in force

lock-out agreement *noun* an agreement under which a seller agrees to keep a property off the market once a price has been agreed with the prospective buyer, to prevent gazumping

lockup *noun* a garage, usually one of several grouped together, that can be rented

loft *noun* **1.** the area between the ceiling of the top floor of a building and the roof **2.** *US* an upper floor of a commercial building such as a factory or warehouse, typically converted for residential or studio use

loft access *noun* a ceiling hatch, staircase or other means of access to a loft

loft apartment *noun* a large apartment on an upper floor of a building, typically with an open-plan layout and in a building converted from industrial use

loft conversion *noun* a conversion that transforms a loft into a habitable room

loft insulation *noun* any of various materials laid between ceiling joists to prevent heat escaping through the roof of a building

loggia *noun* a covered open-sided walkway, often with arches, along one side of a building

London Borough Council *noun* a local authority that administers any of the various London boroughs

London Inter-Bank Offered Rate *noun* an interest rate offered for short-term loans between banks, updated daily

London stock *noun* a type of brick with a slightly irregular finish, suitable for period work, made using an automated moulding process

long lease *noun* a lease that runs for fifty years or more

long residential tenancy *noun* same as **lease**

long-term let *noun* a let for a fairly long period, usually several years

look over *verb* to inspect a property by visiting it and walking round it

loophole *noun* a small mistake or omission in a rule or law that allows it to be circumvented

Loot *noun* a newspaper and website advertising, among other things, properties for sale or rent

loss adjustor *noun* somebody employed by an insurance company to assess the financial losses incurred through an insurable event such as accident, theft, fire, or natural disaster and determine the amount of compensation. Also called **claim adjustor**

lot *noun* **1.** *US* a small area of land that has fixed boundaries **2.** an item or group of items on sale at an auction

lounge *noun* **1.** a sitting room or living room in a house **2.** a couch without a back but with a headrest at one end

louvre *noun* an opening in the form of fixed or moveable slats

low-cost home ownership *noun* any of various schemes designed to provide affordable housing, usually involving part-ownership and part-rental

low-demand housing *noun* housing considered as not meeting the current and future aspirations or potential homebuyers

low-rent *adjective* having a low rental cost

low start mortgage *noun* a mortgage designed to help the borrower keep down the cost of payments in the early years

loyalty bonus *noun* a special discount or privilege offered to people who take out a mortgage with the bank or building society that they have an existing account with

LTV *abbreviation* loan-to-value

lumber *noun* **1.** *US* timber **2.** large objects that are not being used and are stored out of sight

lumen *noun* the unit of luminous flux or visible light

lump sum *noun* an amount of money that is paid in one single payment, not in several small amounts

M

magistrates' court *noun* **1.** a building where magistrates try cases **2.** a court presided over by magistrates

mailing list *noun* a list of names and addresses of people who want to receive information about property as it become available, held by a council or estate agent

mail redirection *noun* a postal service in which post sent to a former address is redirected to a new address

main contractor *noun* the principal contractor on a large construction project, who may subcontract aspects of the construction to other smaller contractors

main residence *noun* a property that is someone's main home

mains *noun* **1.** the central network of pipes or cables that distribute water, gas, or electricity from a local station to individual buildings in an area **2.** if you turn something such as water or gas off at the mains, you turn off the supply to the whole house

mains water *noun* water which comes directly from the mains network

maintenance *noun* **1.** work that is done regularly to keep a building in good condition **2.** the general condition of a property with respect to repairs

maintenance charge *noun* a charge for the upkeep of the shared spaces of a building or its grounds

mairie *noun* (*in France*) a town hall

maître d'oeuvres *noun* (*in France*) a qualified builder

makeover *noun* a remodelling of a building or room that completely changes the way it looks

makeover show *noun* same as **home makeover show**

making time of the essence *noun* a provision in a contract that makes a date stipulated impossible to challenge or overlook

male socket *noun* a socket with pins designed to fit into the holes of a female socket

management company *noun* a company that arranges many of the functions relating to property, e.g. the collection of rents, maintenance and the payment of outgoings

mandat exclusif *noun* (*in France*) an estate agent's exclusive authority to sell a property on behalf of the vendor

mandat simple *noun* (*in France*) an estate agent's authority to sell a property on behalf of the vendor

marae *noun* in New Zealand, an enclosed space or courtyard in front of a house

market *noun* the demand for goods or services being offered for sale. ◊ **property market**

market appraisal *noun* an estate agent's estimate of the value of a property that a client is considering selling

marriage value *noun* the potential for a flat's value to increase when a new lease is granted

masking tape *noun* easy-to-remove adhesive tape used to cover parts of a surface that are not meant to be painted

masonry *noun* **1.** someone who makes the stone parts of buildings and other structures, or who prepares and shapes stone for builders to use **2.** the trade of a mason **3.** the stone or brick parts of a building or other structure

masonry construction *noun* the use of stone as a building material

masonry nails *plural noun* heavy-duty nails designed to be hammered into stone or concrete

mason's mitre *noun* a 90° mitre joint used for masonry mouldings, as distinct from a mitre joint in which each member is cut at 45°

Master Locksmiths' Association *noun* an association established to set and promote standards of conduct, practice and materials within locksmithing

mastic *noun* a flexible cement used as a filler and sealant in woodwork, plaster and brickwork

materials *plural noun* substances out of which objects are produced, e.g. wood, plastic and concrete

matrimonial home *noun* the place where a husband and wife live together

matt *adjective* used for describing paint that has a dull finish with little or no sheen

mattress *noun* **1.** a large pad on which to sleep, usually containing springs or a soft springy filling **2.** a slab or platform used as a foundation for a building **3.** a metal framework inside reinforced concrete

maul *noun* **1.** a large heavy hammer, usually with a wooden head, used for driving in piles, stakes or wedges **2.** a heavy hammer that has one side of the head shaped like a wedge, making it suitable for splitting logs or wood

maximum mortgage period *noun* the maximum repayment period for a home loan, usually 35 years or retirement age

MCB *abbreviation* miniature circuit breaker

MDF *noun* a construction material made by compressing wood fibres into sheets, widely used in furniture, e.g. as the material for the carcasses of kitchen cabinets. Full form **medium density fibreboard**

medallion *noun* a round or oval decoration on something such as a building, vase, or piece of material

mediador autorizado *noun* (*in Portugal*) a state-licensed estate agent

mediatore immobiliare *noun* (*in Italy*) an estate agent

medium density fibreboard *noun* full form of **MDF**

melamine *noun* a type of tough hard plastic widely used as a surface material, e.g. in flat-pack furniture

membrane *noun* a thin, pliable and often porous sheet of any natural or artificial material

memorandum of agreement *noun* a document that formalises an agreement between two parties to work together on a project

memorandum of satisfaction *noun* a document showing that a company has repaid a mortgage or charge (NOTE: The plural is **memoranda**.)

memoria de calidades *noun* (*in Spain*) a set of plans or a detailed specification for a building, usually drawn up by an architect or builder

Messenger-at-Arms *noun* an officer of the Scottish Court of Session, responsible for serving documents and enforcing court orders throughout Scotland

meter *noun* a device installed inside or outside a residential or commercial building to measure the amount of electricity consumed in a specific period

meter reading *noun* **1.** a reading from a gas, electricity or water meter, which shows how many units have been used **2.** a reading produced by an electrical or electronic measuring device, e.g. one recording the extent of dampness in a wall

Metropolitan Borough Council, **Metropolitan District Council** *noun* a large administrative area covering an urban area in England or Wales

mews *noun* **1.** a small street that originally had stables on it but now has houses on it **2.** the houses in a mews

mezzanine *noun* a low storey, especially one between the ground floor and the first floor in a building

miniature circuit breaker *noun* an automatic switch that protects an electrical circuit from damage caused by an overload or short circuit

minimum unexpired lease term *noun* the minimum number of years that must be left on the lease of a leasehold property before a lender will offer a mortgage on it

mining search *noun* a check, conducted on behalf of a prospective housebuyer, for evidence of mining, usually coal mining, in the area of the house, which may lead to concerns over subsidence

minute of waiver *noun* (*in Scotland*) a formal deed containing the renunciation of a right (NOTE: Historically an authority could grant a minute of waiver modifying the conditions of a **feu**.)

MIRAS *abbreviation* mortgage interest relief at source

misrepresentation *noun* the act of making a wrong statement with the intention of persuading someone to enter into a contract

missell *verb* to describe a service or product that you are selling inaccurately, by lies or omission, in order to persuade a person to buy it

missives *plural noun* (*in Scotland*) the exchange of letters between solicitors constituting the contract of sale of property, which, when concluded, constitutes a binding contract

mist coat *noun* a watered-down first coat of paint that is primarily an undercoat but is used for highlighting imperfections in the base for repair

mitre, **mitre joint** *noun* a joint between two members that are cut at an angle of 45°

mobile phone mast *noun* a mast that forms a part of a cellular network operated by a company providing mobile telephone services

modular *adjective* of furniture, made up of separate but matching pieces that can be rearranged, replaced, combined, or interchanged easily

modular home *noun* US a residential property which is built in a central facility and delivered to the proper site fully constructed

money laundering *noun* the act of passing illegal money into the banking system

Money Laundering Regulations 2003 *noun* a piece of UK legislation designed to prevent the use of the financial system for the purpose of money laundering

money transfer *noun* an act of making money available to an individual or institution in another place, carried out by financial institutions but often with a postal or telegraph service as the initiator

monies *noun* money (*formal*)

monkey *noun* the ram of a piledriver

monolith *noun* a large uniform block of a single building material such as concrete pieced together with others to form a building or other structure

mortar *noun* a mixture of sand, water and cement or lime that becomes hard like stone, used in building to hold bricks and stones together ■ *verb* to hold stones and bricks together with mortar

mortarboard *noun* a square board with a handle in the centre of the underside, used by bricklayers for carrying mortar

mortgage *noun* **1.** an agreement in which someone lends money to another person so that he or she can buy a property, the property being used as the security **2.** money lent in this way ■ *verb* to accept a loan with a property as security

mortgage advance *noun* a sum of money given by a financial institution to a customer for the purpose of buying property

mortgage advisor *noun* a professional who give advice on mortgage products to potential buyers. Also called **mortgage broker**, **mortgage intermediary**

mortgage agreement *noun* a lender's agreement to provide a home loan for the purpose of buying a particular property

mortgage agreement in principle *noun* a lender's agreement to provide a home loan to someone who has yet to identify a property he or she would like to buy

mortgage bond *noun* a certificate showing that a mortgage exists and that the property is security for it

mortgage broker *noun* same as **mortgage advisor**

mortgage calculator *noun* a formula or system that prospective mortgage applicants can use for calculating how much they can afford to borrow and how much the repayments will be

Mortgage Conduct of Business Sourcebook *noun* the part of the FSA Handbook that contains the conduct of business rules for mortgage intermediaries and lenders

mortgage debenture *noun* a loan made by a bank to a company for the purpose of buying land or property that is the security for the loan and that the company cannot sell without the permission of the bank

mortgage deed *noun* a legal document setting out the mortgage lender's interest in the property and containing the terms of the mortgage

mortgagee *noun* a person or company that lends money for someone to buy a property that is the security for the loan

mortgage fee *noun* a fee paid by the borrower to cover costs incurred by the lender in securing the loan

mortgage guarantee insurance, mortgage indemnity guarantee, mortgage insurance premium *noun* insurance taken out by a mortgage lender to cover any discrepancy between the value of the loan and the money recovered from the sale of a repossessed property

mortgage intermediary[1] *noun* someone who arranges mortgages on behalf of clients and is not tied to any particular lender

mortgage intermediary[2] *noun* same as **mortgage advisor**

mortgage lender *noun* a business, usually a bank or building society, which offers different types of mortgage loans. Also called **mortgage provider**

mortgage lender's survey *noun* a simple property inspection to establish whether the value of a property corresponds to the amount of the required mortgage loan. This type of survey does not typically highlight any structural defects.

mortgage offer *noun* a lender's official offer to provide a client with a mortgage

mortgage options *plural noun* the various types of home loan that are available

mortgage payment protection insurance *noun* insurance that pays a borrower's monthly mortgage payments should he or she become unable to pay them through unemployment, illness, accident or disability

mortgage payments, mortgage repayments *plural noun* money paid each month as interest on a mortgage, together with repayment of a small part of the capital borrowed

mortgage protection insurance *noun* same as **mortgage payment protection insurance**

mortgage provider *noun* same as **mortgage lender**

mortgage shortfall *noun* the amount by which the value of money obtained from the sale of property is less than the value of the mortgage on it

mortgage subsidy *noun* a payment made by an employer to subsidise the cost of interest payments on an employee's home loan

mortgage term *noun* the number of years over which mortgage payments are made

mortgagor *noun* someone who borrows money, giving a property as security

mortice *noun* a hole or slot cut into a piece of wood, stone, or other material, for a projecting part to be inserted into it, in order to form a tight joint, used in furniture-making and building. ◊ **mortice-and-tenon joint**

mortice-and-tenon joint *noun* a strong joint used in construction and furniture-making which uses a projecting part (a mortice) and a corresponding slot (the tenon) to join two pieces or wood or stone

mortice rackbolt *noun* a bolt on a door that is turned by a key, usually fitted in addition to the door's standard lock

mosaic *noun* a picture or design made with small pieces of coloured material such as glass or tile stuck onto a surface

mould *noun* **1.** a fungus which grows in warm, dark, humid places (NOTE: Mould may accompany leakages or damp problems in a house.) **2.** same as **moulding**

moulding *noun* a feature that is cut or moulded into a decorative shape, e.g. a ceiling cornice or a section of wood panelling

mounting box *noun* a metal or plastic box behind an electrical socket or switch, to which the faceplate fits

movable property *noun* objects of property that can be moved, e.g. furniture, as distinct from buildings and land

movement bead *noun* a metal trim that stabilises two plasterboard surfaces joined at an angle and prevents movement

moving day *noun* the day on which someone moves house, when the removal is carried out

MRICS *abbreviation* Member of the Royal Institution of Chartered Surveyors

multioccupancy dwelling *noun* a residential property occupied by more than one household

multiple agency *noun* a joint agency in which more than two agents are appointed

N

NAEA *abbreviation* National Association of Estate Agents

nail *noun* a strong metal pin with a flat round head and a pointed end that is hammered into wood or masonry and used to fasten objects together or hang something on ■ *verb* to fasten or secure something using nails

NASC *abbreviation* National Access and Scaffolding Confederation

National Access and Scaffolding Confederation *noun* a UK national representative employers' organisation for the access and scaffolding industry. Abbreviation **NASC**

National Approved Letting Scheme *noun* a UK accreditation scheme for lettings and management agents. Abbreviation **NATL**

National Association of Estate Agents *noun* a UK accreditation body for estate agency personnel. Abbreviation **NAEA**

National Association of Realtors *noun* a US accreditation body for realtors

National Conveyancing Protocol *noun* the Law Society's definitive guide to best practice in domestic transactions of freehold and leasehold property

National Debtline *noun* a UK service offering free and confidential advice on how to solve debt problems

National Federation of Builders *noun* a UK accreditation, education and lobbying body for the construction industry. Abbreviation **NFB**

National Federation of Demolition Contractors *noun* a representative body for the UK demolition industry. Abbreviation **NFDC**

National Federation of Residential Landlords *noun* a UK organisation that seeks to ensure high standards of service within the private rented sector and provides a means to resolve disputes between landlords and tenants. Abbreviation **NFRL**

National Federation of Roofing Contractors *noun* a UK representative body for roofing contractors that also provides training and education, technical consulting, business services and market promotion

National Guild of Removers and Storers *noun* a UK representative body for companies involved in the removals and storage industries. Abbreviation **the Guild**

National House Building Council *noun* full form of **NHBC**

National House Building Council Scotland *noun* the Scottish arm of the National House Building Council

National Housing Federation *noun* a UK federation that represents independent housing associations

National Inspection Council for Electrical Installation Contracting *noun* the UK consumer safety organisation and independent regulatory body for the electrical industry. Abbreviation **NICEIC**

National Land Information Service *noun* a UK organisation providing electronic access to all the official sources of land and property information. Abbreviation **NLIS**

National Landlords Association *noun* a UK association that protects and promotes the interests of private-sector residential landlords. Abbreviation **NLA**

National Land Use Database *noun* a UK database that holds data on vacant and derelict sites and produces a comprehensive and up-to-date map of UK land use. Abbreviation **NLUD**

national park *noun* a large area of public land chosen by a government for its scenic, recreational, scientific or historical importance and usually given special protection

National Register of Warranted Builders *noun* a register, held by the Federation of Master Builders, of all builders in the UK who provide a MasterBond warranty against faults in construction. Abbreviation **NRWB**

National Security Inspectorate *noun* a UK approvals body providing inspection services for the security and fire industries. Abbreviation **NSI**

National Trust *noun* a charitable organisation in England, Wales and Northern Ireland concerned with the preservation of areas of great natural beauty and historic buildings and monuments for the benefit of the public. Abbreviation **NT**

Nationwide House Price Index *noun* a monthly review of UK house prices carried out by one of the UK's biggest mortgage lenders

NATL *abbreviation* National Approved Letting Scheme

natural fibre *noun* a fibre such as wool, silk, jute, coir or flax, produced from natural materials

nearby railway schemes *plural noun* details of any plans to build a railway or tramway near a particular property

nearby road schemes *plural noun* details of any plans to build a road near a particular property

needle *noun* **1.** a pointed indicator on a dial, scale or scientific instrument, e.g. a moisture meter **2.** a tall stone pillar **3.** a sharp tool used in engraving **4.** a beam that passes through a wall as a temporary support

negative easement *noun* an easement in which the servient owner stops the dominant owner from doing something

negative equity *noun* a situation in which a property is worth less than the amount that is still owed to the mortgage lender, caused by a sharp fall in property prices after buying

negative equity transfer *noun* the transfer of negative equity on a property being sold to a new property under the terms of a new mortgage

negligence *noun* **1.** failure to give proper care to something, especially a duty or responsibility, with the result that a person or property is harmed **2.** the offence of acting carelessly towards others so as to cause harm, entitling the injured party to claim damages

negotiator *noun* someone who carries on discussions with the aim of reaching an agreement

neighbourhood *noun* a residential area in which someone lives

neighbourhood renewal *noun* changes made to the built environment in an area in order to improve the quality of life there

neighbourhood renewal fund *noun* a UK government fund established to assist with neighbourhood renewal

neighbourhood watch scheme *noun* a UK crime prevention initiative in which groups of local residents implement crime prevention measures and liaise with police in monitoring their local area

nemo dat quod non habet *phrase* the rule that no one can pass or sell to another person something such as stolen goods to which he or she has no title, the Latin phrase literally meaning 'no one can give what he does not have'

new build, new-build *noun* a property which has been recently constructed and has often not previously been occupied

newel post *noun* a post that is the part of a staircase to which the banister is fitted

new home warranty scheme *noun* a UK scheme in which a warranty is given when a final full inspection of a newly constructed home is completed satisfactorily, before funds are released by the lender

NFB *abbreviation* National Federation of Builders

NFDC *abbreviation* National Federation of Demolition Contractors

NFRC *abbreviation* National Federation of Roofing Contractors

NFRL *abbreviation* National Federation of Residential Landlords

NHBC *noun* the standard-setting body and leading warranty and insurance provider for new and newly converted homes in the UK. Full form **National House Building Council**

NICEIC *abbreviation* National Inspection Council for Electrical Installation Contracting

99-year lease *noun* a lease for a flat that was bought from a local authority before the introduction of the Housing Act 1980, the terms of which vary greatly from authority to authority and are sometimes negotiated individually

NLA *abbreviation* National Landlords Association

NLIS *abbreviation* National Land Information Service

NLUD *abbreviation* National Land Use Database

no-claims discount *noun* a discount on the cost of insurance for customers who have not made claims over a given number of years

nog *noun* **1.** a block of wood inserted into masonry or brickwork so that something can be nailed to it **2.** a wooden peg or pin

nogging *noun* **1.** small stones, bricks or bits of masonry used to fill the spaces between studs in a wall or partition **2.** one of the pieces of wood inserted between the main timbers of a half-timbered wall

Noise Abatement Society *noun* an association of people who work to influence others to reduce noise

Noise Act *noun* a piece of UK legislation that addresses problems created by noise emitted from residential properties at night

noise control *noun* measures taken to limit noise emitted, e.g. from properties

noise pollution *noun* noise that causes discomfort

nominee *noun* a person or group that holds title to a property but is not the true owner

non-domestic rates *plural noun* same as **business rates**

non-fossil fuels *plural noun* ways of generating electricity other than by burning coal and natural gas, such as solar panels

non-owning occupier *noun* a tenant

non-owning spouse *noun* someone who is married to or cohabiting with a person who is the owner of a property that both live in

non-profit making organisation *noun* an organisation that exists in order to provide services from which it makes no profit, which are eligible for various types of relief, e.g. from council tax or business rates

non-residential property *noun* a property that is not used as a dwelling

Non-resident Landlords Scheme *noun* a UK government scheme for taxing the UK rental income of landlords resident overseas

non-status mortgage *noun* a mortgage for individuals who do not have proof of income, e.g. freelancers, commission workers and self-employed people

no sale, no fee conveyancing *noun* conveyancing services for which a client does not pay if the sale of property is not completed

nosing *noun* **1.** the rounded edge of a stair tread that projects horizontally **2.** a shield that protects a nosing on a staircase **3.** the rounded projecting edge of an architectural moulding

notaio *noun* (*in Italy*) a notary

notaire *noun* (*in France*) a notary

notano *noun* (*in Portugal*) a notary

notario *noun* (*in Spain*) a notary

notary *noun* a person who is legally authorised to certify the authenticity or legitimacy of signatures and documents (NOTE: In many European countries a notary is involved in drawing up contracts for property transactions.)

nota simple *noun* (*in Spain*) a property register

note de renseignement d'urbanisme *noun* (*in France*) a document that provides details of all the planning rules applicable to a particular property

notice *noun* **1.** the period of time between the giving of a warning or notification and its taking effect **2.** official notification of the exercise of a right, especially the right to terminate employment, or the amount of time in advance that such notification is given

notice of title *noun* (*in Scotland*) a formal document that sets out the right to heritable property

notice to quit *noun* formal notice served by a landlord on a tenant before proceedings are started for possession

noting of interest *noun* an indication of interest in a property for sale, lodged with a selling agent on behalf of a client by a solicitor or conveyancer

no title guarantee *noun* a situation in which the title to property being sold is not guaranteed, e.g. because the title deeds have been lost

NRWB *abbreviation* National Register of Warranted Builders

NSI *abbreviation* National Security Inspectorate

NT *abbreviation* National Trust

nuisance *noun* something not allowed by law because it causes harm or offence, either to people in general or to an individual person

nursery *noun* a child's bedroom or playroom in a house

O

objection *noun* a reason for a feeling or expression of opposition

obligations *plural noun* actions that are legally required under the terms of a contract, usually incurring a penalty if not fulfilled

obligatory insurance *noun* insurance that someone is legally obliged to take out

occupancy *noun* **1.** the act of occupying a property **2.** same as **occupation**

occupant *noun* a person who occupies a property

occupation *noun* **1.** the fact of occupying a property that has no owner and thereby acquiring title to the property. Also called **occupancy 2.** the work that someone does

occupier *noun* someone who lives in a property

occupier's liability *noun* the duty of an occupier to make sure that visitors to a property are not harmed

Occupier's Liability Act *noun* a piece of UK legislation that sets out the duty of care an owner of property owes to people he or she has not invited or permitted to be on the property, e.g. trespassers

occupy *verb* **1.** to be living in a property, legally **2.** to enter and stay in a property illegally

offer *verb* to present a property for sale or rent

offer of advance *noun* a document outlining the terms and conditions under which a lender is prepared to lend money

offers over *phrase* (*in Scotland*) used in an invitation to submit offers to buy a property above a stated amount

offer to purchase *noun US* an official offer made in writing to the seller of a property

office copy entries *plural noun* copies of Land Registry documents that prove ownership or property and set out any encumbrances on the land

Office for the Supervision of Solicitors *noun* a UK government office that examines complaints against solicitors

Office of Fair Trading *noun* a UK government department that protects consumers against unfair or illegal business. Abbreviation **OFT**

offset mortgage *noun* a mortgage that allows a borrower to link a mortgage to a savings or current account, thus offsetting the mortgage against another pot of cash

offshore banking *noun* the operation of a bank account with a financial institution in an overseas country, usually for the purpose of tax avoidance

off street parking *noun* the existence of parking spaces in areas that are not public roads, e.g. in driveways and car parks

off the market *phrase* no longer being offered for sale

OFT *abbreviation* Office of Fair Trading

ombudsman *noun* **1.** someone, especially a man, responsible for investigating and resolving complaints from consumers or other members of the public against a company, institution, or other organisation **2.** a UK government official responsible for impartially investigating citizens' complaints against a public authority or institution and trying to bring about a fair settlement

Ombudsman for Estate Agents *noun* a UK service for dealing with disputes between member agencies and customers who are buying and selling residential property

100% mortgage *noun* a mortgage in which the amount of money borrowed is the full cost of the property bought

125-year lease *noun* a standard modern lease for a flat bought from a local authority under the Right to Buy Scheme introduced with the passing of the Housing Act 1980

online calculator *noun* an online service that helps potential mortgage applicants calculate how much they can afford to borrow

ono *abbreviation* or nearest offer

on the market *phrase* available for sale

onward chain *noun* a situation in which a sale of property depends on the seller's purchase of a new property being completed

open market *noun* a market in which anyone can buy or sell

open market HomeBuy *noun* a government scheme that provides someone renting a council or housing association property with an equity loan equivalent to 25% of the purchase price of a property on the open market, repaid with 25% of the value of the property at the time it is resold

open-plan *adjective* used for describing a home or workspace that is not divided into separate rooms in the traditional way but has large spaces combining features of more than one room

open-plan living *noun* the fact of having a residential property with an open-plan layout

operative words *plural noun* words in a conveyancing document that transfer the land or create an interest in the land

option agreement *noun* an agreement to buy a property at a future time, secured by a potential buyer who cannot afford to buy at the time in return for a fee paid to the potential seller who agrees not to sell before a stipulated date

Ordnance Survey *noun* a UK agency that generates accurate mapping data for Great Britain. Abbreviation **OS**

Organisation for Timeshare in Europe *noun* an organisation established to improve representation for reputable companies in the timeshare sector and promote fair trading within the timeshare industry

oriel window *noun* a window that projects from an upper storey wall

or nearest offer *phrase* an indication that a seller will accept the best offer to buy from several potential buyers offering less than the asking price

OS *abbreviation* Ordnance Survey

other income *noun* sources of income that are not someone's main income, such as investments or a second property which brings in rent

ouster *noun* the removal of an occupier from a property so that he or she has to sue to regain possession, used especially in matrimonial proceedings against a violent spouse

outbuilding *noun* a barn, shed, or other structure that is situated away from the main building on a property

outgoing *adjective* in the process of departing or going out of a building or place

outhouse *noun* a small building situated near the main building on a property

outline planning permission *noun* general permission to build a property on a piece of land, not final because there are no details provided

outright acceptance *noun* (*in Scotland*) acceptance by the seller of an offer to purchase, with no further negotiation

outside lighting *noun* lighting that illuminates exterior areas

outstanding notices *plural noun* orders to take action relating to property that the seller has not yet addressed at the time of the sale .

overbuild *verb* **1.** to construct more buildings than are necessary or desirable in an area **2.** to construct something that is too large or elaborate **3.** to build something on top of a particular place or thing

overcoat *noun* an additional protective layer of something such as paint or varnish on top of a treated surface

overdevelop *verb* to develop previously open land to excess

overflow *noun* an outlet that allows water to escape from a tank or a system of pipes if the level becomes dangerously high

overhang *noun* an edge of a roof that projects out over the walls beneath

overhead door *noun* a door that is opened by being lifted vertically, e.g. some garage doors

overlook *verb* of a property or room, to have a view of something

overpaid funds *plural noun* mortgage payments made, usually erroneously, that exceed the value of the loan plus interest

overreaching *noun* a legal principle whereby an interest in land can be replaced by a direct right to money

overriding interest *noun* an interest that comes before that of another party

overseas mortgage *noun* a mortgage with an overseas lender obtained for the purpose of buying a home overseas

oversite *noun* those parts of a structure that are built above ground

own *verb* to have something as your property

owner *noun* someone who owns something

owner-occupier *noun* someone who owns the property that he or she occupies

P

paint *noun* a coloured liquid applied to a surface in order to decorate or protect it

painter *noun* someone whose job is to cover paint the interiors of buildings

pale *noun* **1.** a pointed slat of wood for a fence **2.** a fence marking a boundary

paling *noun* a fence formed by a line of pointed stakes planted in the ground

palisade *noun* **1.** a fence made of pales driven into the ground **2.** a pale in a fence

pallet *noun* **1.** a standardised platform or open-ended box, usually made of wood, that allows mechanical handling of bulk goods during transport and storage **2.** a straw-filled mattress

pane *noun* **1.** a glazed section of a window or door **2.** a piece of plate glass in a window or door **3.** a distinct section of a surface such as a door or wall

panel *noun* **1.** a flat rectangular piece of hard material that serves as a part of something such as a door or wall, often raised above or sunk in the surface **2.** a section between two posts in a fence or gate ∎ *verb* to cover interior walls with wooden panels

paperhanger *noun* someone who hangs wallpaper, especially as a profession

parapet *noun* a low protective wall built where there is a sudden dangerous drop, e.g. along the edge of a balcony, roof or bridge

parcel *noun* a separate and identifiable unit of land in one ownership

parcela *noun* (*in Spain*) a unit of vacant land

parcelle *noun* (*in France*) a plot of land

parget

parget *noun* **1.** plaster, whitewash, roughcast or any similar material used to coat walls or line chimneys **2.** ornamental plasterwork on a wall ■ *verb* to cover walls, line chimneys or decorate a surface with parget

parking dispensation *noun* temporary permission to park in a place or at a time normally outlawed under existing parking restrictions

parking permit *noun* a permit allowing a motorist to park in an area of restricted parking

parking restriction *noun* a rule restricting parking to certain times of day or to motorists who have a parking permit

parking suspension *noun* a rule which 'reserves' a parking spot for one person's use for a particular length of time, to allow something such as a removal van or skip to be parked there

parking suspension permit *noun* a permit enforcing a parking suspension (NOTE: Permits to suspend parking outside a property to facilitate removal vehicles or skips can be obtained from your local authority.)

part and part mortgage *noun* a mortgage in which part of the loan is paid on a repayment basis and part on an interest-only basis

part endowment mortgage *noun* a mortgage in which part of the loan is paid by means of an endowment

part exchange scheme *noun* a scheme in which a developer undertakes to sell the existing home of the buyer of one of its new properties, the purchase of which is partly funded from the sale of the existing home

particle board *noun US* any manufactured board made by gluing wood particles of varying size together under pressure. Chipboard and flakeboard are types of particle board.

particular lien *noun* the right of a person to keep possession of another person's property until debts relating to that property have been paid

particulars of sale *plural noun* a part of a contract of sale of property that describes the property and gives details of the lease or freehold

partition *noun* the division of land that is held by joint tenants or tenants in common

partition wall *noun* a wall that divides an area into two rooms but does not support any of the weight of the building. Compare **load-bearing wall**

part-ownership *noun* a situation in which two or more persons own the same property

party wall *noun* a wall that separates two adjoining properties and belongs to both owners equally

Party Wall etc Act 1996 *noun* a piece of UK legislation that sets out the procedure to follow when building work involves a party wall

passive solar heating *noun* methods of building design and positioning that are designed to maximise the natural heating effect of the sun

patio *noun* a paved area adjoining a house, used for outdoor dining and recreation

patrimonio *noun* (*in Spain*) wealth tax

pavement *noun* **1.** a paved path for pedestrians alongside a street **2.** material that is used to make a pavement, e.g. concrete or stone **3.** the layered structure that forms the surface of a path, road or aircraft runway

pavement vehicle access *noun* the provision of dropped kerbs or crossovers

paver *noun* **1.** a stone or slab used to pave an area such as a patio **2.** someone who installs or lays a pavement

pavilion *noun* a largely ornamental building in a park or garden, used for shelter and entertainment

paving *noun* **1.** a firm usually flat surface made of stone, brick, concrete or other material **2.** material used for making a firm hard surface, e.g. concrete or stones **3.** the act of making a paved surface

pavior, paviour *noun* **1.** a stone, slab or block used to pave an outdoor area such as a patio **2.** someone whose occupation is laying external paving

payment protection insurance *noun* same as **mortgage payment protection insurance**

Peabody Trust *noun* a major charitable trust and housing association in London

pea gravel *noun* gravel consisting of fairly small rounded stones, used for concrete or as a pathway or driveway surface

pebbledash *noun* a finish for exterior walls, consisting of small stones set in plaster

pecuniary *adjective* involving a financial penalty such as a fine

penalty-free mortgage *noun* a mortgage agreement in which there is no penalty for early repayment

pendant *noun* **1.** a lamp, chandelier or other lighting fixture that hangs from the ceiling **2.** an architectural ornament hanging from a vaulted ceiling or roof

pending action *noun* a court action that has not yet been heard

penetrating damp *noun* dampness that penetrates a building from outside, as distinct from rising damp

pension *noun* **1.** a fixed amount of money paid regularly to someone during retirement by the government, a former employer or through an annuity **2.** a sum of money paid regularly as compensation, e.g. for an injury sustained on a job

pension mortgage *noun* an interest-only mortgage in which payments are made into a pension fund, rather than an endowment fund. Also called **personal pension plan mortgage**

penthouse *noun* **1.** a large and usually luxurious apartment on the top floor of a building, usually one commanding an impressive view **2.** a structure on the roof of a building that houses lift machinery, a water tank or other service equipment

penthouse apartment, penthouse flat *noun* same as **penthouse**

peppercorn rent *noun* a very small or nominal rent

percolation test *noun* a test conducted on land to check the efficiency of its natural drainage

periodic tenancy *noun* a tenancy in which the tenant rents for several short periods but not for a fixed length of time

period property *noun* an old property built in the architectural style typical of a particular period

peristyle *noun* **1.** a row of columns that encircles a building or a courtyard **2.** a building or courtyard that has a peristyle

permanent residency *noun* the status of someone who has been granted permission to live indefinitely in a country of which he or she is not a citizen

permanent resident *noun* someone with permanent residency

permis de construire *noun* (*in France*) planning permission

permiso de edificar *noun* (*in Spain*) a building permit

permissive waste *noun* damage to a property that is caused by a tenant not carrying out repairs

perpetuity *noun* **1.** the transfer of property for an unlimited period of time (NOTE: The maximum legal period of transferred ownership is based on the length of a life in existence at the time plus 21 years plus a nine month period of gestation.) **2.** an investment with no maturity date, designed to pay an annual return indefinitely

personal chattels *plural noun* household things such as furniture, clothes or cars that belong to a person and are not land

personal estate *noun* the set of things, excluding land, that belong to someone and can be inherited by their heirs

personal loan *noun* a loan to a person for household or other personal use, not for business use

personal pension plan mortgage *noun* same as **pension mortgage**

personal property *noun* property that belongs to one person, excluding land and buildings, but including items such as money, goods and securities

personal protective equipment *noun* any device to be worn or held by an individual for protection against one or more health and safety risks. Abbreviation **PPE**

personal representative *noun* **1.** a person who is the executor of a will or the administrator of the estate of a deceased person. Abbreviation **pr 2.** a person appointed to deal with the estate of a person who dies intestate

personalty *noun* personal property or chattels as distinct from land

pest control *noun* the process of keeping down the number of pests by various methods

pest controller *noun* someone whose work involves the control or elimination of pests such as rats and cockroaches

phased development *noun* development that proceeds in phases, with properties becoming occupied at the end of each phase

phasing *noun* same as **stage payments**

physical search *noun* a search of written documents, as distinct from a computer search

piazza *noun* a covered passageway that has arches on one or both sides and is usually attached to a building, e.g. along the inner walls of a courtyard or quadrangle

picket *noun* a post or plank with a pointed end that is hammered into the ground, e.g. as a marker or as a support for a fence

pièce de garantie *noun* (*in France*) a bond guaranteeing the protection of a purchaser's deposit

pier *noun* **1.** a pillar, especially a rectangular one supporting the end of an arch, lintel or vault **2.** an area of wall between two adjacent doors, windows or other openings **3.** a column of masonry projecting from a wall **4.** a vertical structure, usually of masonry, built against a wall to support it

pile *noun* **1.** a vertical wood, metal or concrete support for a building or other structure that is driven into the ground. Also called **piling 2.** the surface of a carpet or of a fabric such as velvet that is formed of short, sometimes cut, loops of fibre ■ *verb* to use piles as a support for a building or other structure

piledriver *noun* a large mechanical hammering device that uses steam, compressed air or gravity to drive construction piles into the ground

piling *noun* **1.** the driving of piles into the ground for structural support **2.** piles driven into the ground, considered collectively **3.** a structure built of piles **4.** same as **pile**

pillar *noun* a vertical column that is part of a building or other structure and can be either a support or decoration

pilot light, pilot *noun* a small gas flame that remains lit in order to ignite a burner when it is turned on

pipe insulation *noun* the use of various materials to protect pipes from frost damage and prevent heat from escaping from them

pipework *noun* a system of pipes

pitch *noun* **1.** a dark sticky substance obtained from tar and used in the building trade, especially for waterproofing roofs **2.** the angle of slope of a roof expressed in degrees **3.** the highest point of something such as an arch

pitched roof *noun* a traditional roof, with sloping surfaces, as distinct from a flat roof

pitcher *noun* a paving stone, especially one made of granite

plaintiff *noun* someone who starts an action against someone in the civil courts. Compare **defendant** (NOTE: Since the introduction of the new Civil Procedure Rules in April 1999, this term has been replaced by **claimant**.)

plan *noun* **1.** a drawing or diagram on a horizontal plane of the layout or arrangement of something **2.** a scale drawing showing the various perspectives of something, especially a building ■ *verb* to make a scale drawing of something, especially a building

plan cadastral *noun* (*in France*) the registered plan of a property

plan de bornage, plan d'arpentage *noun* (*in France*) a plan that identifies a property's boundaries

plan general de ordenación urbana *noun* (*in Spain*) a town plan that indicates how land is zoned

plank *noun* **1.** a long flat piece of timber sawn thicker than a board **2.** a piece of preformed concrete in the shape of a wooden plank, used for construction ■ *verb* to cover something with planks

planking *noun* **1.** planks used as building material **2.** the work of covering something with planks or laying planks

Planning Act *noun* same as **Town and Country Planning Act**

Planning Advisory Service *noun* a service that provides support and encouragement to local authority planning departments

Planning and Compulsory Purchase Act *noun* a piece of UK legislation designed to make the planning system in England and Wales more flexible and responsive to local needs

planning approval *noun* initial approval in principle of a planning application, which does not constitute permission to begin building work. Compare **planning permission**

planning authority *noun* a local body, typically a local authority, that gives permission for changes to be made to existing buildings or for new use of land

planning consent *noun* same as **planning permission**

planning control *noun* official regulations which govern the development and use of land

Planning Inspectorate *noun* a UK government agency that processes planning and enforcement appeals and holds inquiries into local development plans

planning permission *noun* an official document allowing a person or company to plan new buildings on empty land or to alter existing buildings. Also called **planning consent** (NOTE: Planning permission is granted by a Local Authority and must be applied for if you are planning significant changes to the outside of your property or if it is being divided into separate homes or business premises. Restrictions may apply for listed buildings and those located in conservation areas. The LA will also consider any impact the work may have on your neighbours and on the use of local utilities such as roads.)

planning policy guidance notes *plural noun* statements of the government's national policy and principles towards certain aspects of the town planning framework

Planning Portal *noun* a UK government online planning and building regulations resource, holding information on planning and building regulations, and receiving applications for planning permission and building regulations consent

plant *noun* heavy machinery, vehicles and other equipment used in construction work

plant hire *noun* the hire of heavy machinery, vehicles and other equipment for use in construction work

plaster *noun* a mixture of lime, sand†and water that is applied as a liquid paste to the ceilings and internal walls of a building and dries to a hard surface ▪ *verb* to apply plaster to the interior walls and ceilings of a building

plaster bead *noun* a metal trim used to reinforce a plasterboard wall

plasterboard *noun* reinforced gypsum plaster sandwiched between two layers of strong paper in large sheets, used chiefly for interior walls

plasterwork *noun* objects in plaster, especially the layer of plaster applied to interior wall surfaces or decorative plaster mouldings on ceilings or walls

plasticiser *noun* a substance added to a concrete or mortar mix to make it more workable

plate *noun* **1.** a thin flat rigid sheet or slice of some material, usually of uniform thickness and with a smooth surface **2.** a piece, sheet or slab of flat metal used to join or strengthen things **3.** a horizontal timber laid along the top of a wall of a building to support the ends of timbers laid at right angles to the wall

platform *noun* a simple structure, especially one composed of wooden planks, serving as a base for keeping things clear of the ground

plinth *noun* **1.** a square block beneath a column, pedestal or statue **2.** the part of the wall of a building immediately above the ground, usually a course of stones or bricks. Also called **plinth course 3.** the square block at the base on each side of a doorframe

plot *noun* **1.** a small piece of ground **2.** *US* an architectural plan of a building or estate ▪ *verb US* to make a plan or map of something such as a building or estate

plumb in *verb* to install something by fitting the system of pipes needed to allow it to work

plumbing *noun* **1.** the work that a plumber does **2.** the pipes and fixtures that carry or use water or gas in a building

plusvalía *noun* (*in Spain*) a local capital gains tax

plus value *noun* (*in France*) capital gains tax

podium *noun* a low wall forming a foundation or base, e.g. for a colonnade

point *verb* to repair or finish a wall, chimney or other structural component by putting mortar or cement between the bricks or stones

pointing *noun* **1.** the cement or mortar between the bricks of a wall **2.** the act of repairing or finishing a wall by putting mortar or cement between the bricks

pole scabbler *noun* a pneumatic pole-shaped tool used for giving a rough keyed surface to concrete on which further construction is to take place

policy document *noun* a document that sets out the terms of an insurance policy

polyvinyl chloride *noun* full form of **PVC**

porch *noun* a covered shelter at the entrance to a building

portable mortgage *noun* a mortgage that can be transferred without penalty if the borrower moves house during the repayment period

portico *noun* **1.** a covered entrance to a large building **2.** a covered walkway, often leading to the main entrance of a building, that consists of a roof supported by pillars

portion *noun* money or property given to a young person to provide money for them as income

positive covenant *noun* an agreement between a buyer or seller, or a tenant and landlord, in which one party agrees to take some action in relation to the other party

possession *noun* **1.** control over property **2.** physically holding something that does not necessarily belong to you

possession in law *noun* ownership of land or buildings without actually occupying them

possessions register *noun* a register of people whose homes have been repossessed on a voluntary or involuntary basis

possessive action *noun* a court action brought with the intention of regaining possession of land or buildings

possessory *adjective* referring to possession of property

possessory title *noun* a title to land acquired by occupying it continuously, usually for twelve years

post *noun* **1.** a pole of wood or metal fixed in the ground in an upright position, serving as a support, marker or place for attaching things **2.** a vertical piece in a building frame that supports a beam **3.** one of the upright supports of a piece of furniture such as a chair or a four-poster bed

post and beam *noun* a method of construction in which structural support is provided by large, widely spaced wooden members that are usually visible inside or outside the structure

postcode *noun* a series of numbers and letters that forms part of an address, indicating the street and the town in a way that can be read by a scanner

post-contract *adjective* taking place after a contract has been signed

post redirection *noun* same as **mail redirection**

post-tensioned concrete *noun* concrete to which tension is applied by hydraulic jacks after it has hardened

power line, power cable *noun* a wire, carried across the countryside on pylons, along which electric current travels from the power station where it was generated

power of appointment *noun* a power given to one person such as a trustee to dispose of property belonging to another

power of attorney *noun* an official power giving someone the right to act on someone else's behalf in legal matters

power shower *noun* a shower with a powerful flow of water delivered by a pump

power supplier *noun* a company supplying electricity or gas to domestic and business customers

power supply *noun* a mains supply of electricity

PPE *abbreviation* personal protective equipment

precast concrete *noun* concrete cast into blocks or units for use in construction projects, as distinct from semiliquid concrete used for pouring. Also called **prefabricated reinforced concrete**

precept *noun* **1.** a warrant or writ that is issued by a legal authority **2.** an order for the payment of money

precepting body *noun* an organisation that levies a precept

pre-completion *adjective* relating to the period before the completion of the sale of property

pre-contract *noun* a contract made in advance to prevent a subsequent contract ■ *verb* to make a contract or enter into an agreement in advance

prefabricate *verb* to manufacture sections of something, especially a building, that can be transported to a site and easily assembled there

prefabricated materials *plural noun* construction materials or members assembled before they are delivered to the construction site

prefabricated reinforced concrete *noun* same as **precast concrete**

preferred contractor *noun* a contractor on a list of those recommended by a local authority

preliminary inquiries *plural noun* an initial letter from the prospective buyer's solicitor to the vendor's solicitor asking about the vendor's title to the property

Premier Guarantee a trade name for a new home warranty scheme

premises *plural noun* **1.** a building, considered with or without the land that surrounds it **2.** building and the land it stands on

premium *noun* **1.** a sum of money paid by one person to another, especially one paid regularly **2.** the amount to be paid to a landlord or a tenant for the right to take over a lease **3.** a higher charge for something that is of very good quality

prescription *noun* a presumption of the right of possession of property, based on long-term exercise of property rights

preservation order *noun* a court order that prevents a building from being demolished or a tree from being cut down

preserved right to buy *noun* a right to buy a property given to people who were tenants in properties previously owned by a local authority and now owned by a housing association

pressure cleaner *noun* same as **pressure washer**

pressured-area status *noun* (*in Scotland*) the status of a housing area in which there is a shortage of social housing and the local authority has been granted the right to withdraw housing from the Right-To-Buy Scheme

pressure relief valve *noun* a valve through which excess pressure in a fluid system can escape

pressure washer *noun* a piece of electrical equipment that cleans surfaces such as brickwork by means of a powerful jet of water pumped through a lance-shaped attachment. Also called **pressure cleaner**

prestressed concrete *noun* concrete that is cast over cables that are under tension, so as to increase its strength

presupuesto *noun* (*in Spain*) a quotation for building work

previous lender's reference *noun* a document from a mortgage applicant's previous lender that confirms his or her previous repayment record

previously developed land *noun* same as **brownfield land**

prime *verb* **1.** to prepare a surface for painting or a similar process by treating it with a sealant or an undercoat of paint **2.** to put liquid in something such as a pump in order to get it started

primer *noun* a paint or sealant used to prepare a surface for painting or a similar process

principal *noun* **1.** the initial sum of money invested or borrowed, before interest or other revenue is added, or the remainder of that sum after payments have been made **2.** someone for whom a representative or proxy acts in a legal matter **3.** the main support beam, girder or truss in a roof, bridge or other construction

principal and interest mortgage *noun* a mortgage repaid using the repayment method

principal contractor *noun* same as **main contractor**

principal private dwellinghouse *noun* same as **main residence**

private landlord *noun* a landlord who is a private individual, not, e.g., a local authority or a housing association. Also called **private sector landlord**

private property *noun* property that belongs to a private person, not to the public

private residence relief *noun* tax relief designed to ensure that most people do not pay capital gains tax when they sell their home to move to another

private road *noun* a road that is not maintained by a local authority but by the owner or owners of properties adjacent to it

private sale *noun* a sale of property in which the buyer deals directly with the seller, not with an estate agent

private sector landlord *noun* same as **private landlord**

privity *noun* **1.** a legally recognised relationship between two parties, e.g. between members of a family, between an employer and employees, or between others who have entered into a contract together **2.** a successive or mutual relationship to some property

privity of contract *noun* a relationship between the parties to a contract, which makes the contract enforceable between them

Proceeds of Crime Act 2002 *noun* a piece of UK legislation that places obligations on professionals involved in financial matters with regard to the prevention of money laundering

proceeds of sale *plural noun* money obtained from the sale of property of any kind

professional let *noun* a letting of property to a professional person

profit à prendre *noun* a right to take from land or a river passing through it something such as game or fish

project manager *noun* the manager in charge of a construction project

promesse de vente *noun* (*in France*) a type of preliminary contract in which the seller offers to sell the stated property at a stated price to a stated person within a stated period

promesse synallagmatique de vente *noun* same as **compromis de vente**

proof of identity *noun* a document that proves someone's identity, e.g. a passport

proof of income *noun* a document that proves the level of someone's income, e.g. a payslip or a set of audited accounts

proof of title *noun* a document that proves ownership of property, e.g. a title deed

property *noun* 1. things that are owned by someone 2. land and buildings 3. a building such as a house, shop or factory ■ *adjective* relating to land and buildings

property broker *noun* a professional who is not an estate agent but arranges the sale and purchase of property on behalf of clients

property enquiry certificate *noun* (*in Scotland*) a document produced by a local authority to collate various elements of information about the status of a property, e.g. planning applications and building warrants relating to it

property income taxation *noun* tax paid on income received from renting out property

property information form *noun* a summary of information that will go into the draft contract of sale, provided to allow buyer and seller to check its accuracy

property investment scheme *noun* a scheme, run by a private company, that offers private investors the chance to make a profit by buying, individually or with others, properties that are to be rented out

property management *noun* the business of looking after a property or group of properties on a day-to-day basis on a landlord's behalf (NOTE: Property management usually covers daily maintenance, site visits and monitoring accounts and payments.)

property manager *noun* a person who undertakes property management on behalf of a landlord

property market *noun* 1. the market in letting commercial properties (NOTE: Factors that affect the property market in an area include: economic trends, the numbers of new builds coming onto the market, mortgage availability, planning regulations, social trends such as divorce rates and the number of first-time buyers.) 2. the market in developing commercial properties as investments 3. the process of buying or selling residential properties by individual homeowners

Property Misdescriptions Act 1991 *noun* a piece of UK legislation introduced to prohibit the making of false or misleading claims about property in the course of carrying out real estate business

property open-ended investment company *noun* a company whose business is investment in property

property portfolio diversification *noun* the activity of an investor in property purchasing several investments across a range of property markets

property price survey *noun* a review of property prices produced by any of various companies and institutions, on a monthly or quarterly basis

property register *noun* any of various lists of properties in an area, e.g. a list held by a local authority or by the Land Registry

property tax *noun* a tax levied when a house or other property is sold

property unit trust *noun* a unit trust in which the assets are properties

proposta d'acquisto irrevocabile *noun* (*in Italy*) a written offer to purchase a property, binding on the purchaser's part for a specified period

proprietary *adjective* relating to the ownership of property

proprietary right *noun* the right of someone who owns a property

proprietor *noun* the owner of a property

proprietorship *noun* the fact of being the proprietor of land

proprietorship register *noun* a land register that shows the details of owners of land

protected tenancy *noun* a tenancy in which the tenant is protected from eviction

protected tenant *noun* a tenant who has lived in a rented property for a number of years and has some rights that are not available to short-term tenants

protective goggles *plural noun* goggles worn by tradesmen and building contractors to protect the eyes

protraction *noun* the act of drawing something such as a building or an area of land to scale, or a drawing of this kind

provvigione *noun* (*in Italy*) an estate agent's commission, some of which is paid by the purchaser

public domain *noun* the fact that land, property or information belongs to and is available to the public

public liability insurance *noun* insurance for a business against claims by members of the public

public right of way *noun* minor public highways such as footpaths and bridleways that exist for the benefit of the community at large

public sector landlord *noun* a landlord such as local authority or a housing association

pug *verb* **1.** to mix clay with water to make it pliable enough to form bricks or pottery **2.** to fill in a gap with clay or mortar

puisne mortgage *noun* a mortgage in which the deeds of the property have not been deposited with the lender

pull down *verb* **1.** to destroy or demolish something, especially a building **2.** to reduce something such as a price to a lower level or value

pull out *verb* to withdraw from an obligation or commitment

purchase deed *noun* a document, prepared by the buyer's solicitor, that will legally transfer the property from the seller to the buyer

purchase price *noun* a price paid for something

purchaser *noun* a person or company that buys something

purpose built *adjective* of a property, designed for a specific use or to meet specific needs, e.g. with facilities for the disabled

pursuer *noun* (*in Scotland*) a plaintiff in a lawsuit, who brings a case against the defendant

putty *noun* **1.** a paste with the consistency of dough, made from linseed oil and powdered chalk, used to fix glass into wooden window frames and to fill holes in wood **2.** a thin paste of lime, water and sand or plaster of Paris used as a finishing coat on plaster ■ *verb* to fix windows into wooden frames, or fill holes in wood, using putty

PVC *noun* a type of plastic that is not biodegradable, used for floor coverings and pipes. Full form **polyvinyl chloride**

pylon *noun* **1.** a tall metal tower, typically made of crisscrossing steel bars, that supports high-voltage cables across a long span **2.** a tall vertical structure on or forming part of a building or other construction, especially an ancient structure, e.g. a decorative gateway or a monumental pillar

Q

quadrangle *noun* **1.** an open rectangular yard that is surrounded on all four sides by buildings **2.** the buildings that surround an open rectangular yard

qualified acceptance *noun* (*in Scotland*) initial acceptance by the seller of a prospective buyer's offer to buy a property, subject to further conditions and negotiation, not binding until the missives are concluded

qualified title *noun* a title to a property that is not absolute because there is some defect

quantity surveyor *noun* someone who assesses the cost of a construction job based on the amount of labour and materials required to complete it

quiet enjoyment *noun* the right of an occupier to occupy property peacefully under a tenancy without the landlord or anyone else interfering with that right

quoin *noun* **1.** the outer corner of a wall **2.** a stone block used to form a quoin, especially when it is different, e.g. in size or material, from the other blocks or bricks in the wall **3.** same as **keystone** ■ *verb* to build an outer corner of a wall using blocks that are different, e.g. in size or texture, from the other blocks or bricks used to build the wall

quotation *noun* an estimated price for a job or service. Also called **estimate, quote**

quote *noun* same as **quotation** ■ *verb* to give an estimate of the price of providing someone with a product or service

R

rack rent *noun* **1.** full yearly rent of a property let on a normal lease **2.** a very high rent

radiator *noun* a room-heating device that emits heat from pipes through which hot water, steam, or hot oil circulates, especially one connected to a central boiler-fed system

radon gas *noun* poisonous gas that seeps into homes from radioactive rocks beneath

raft *noun* a thick concrete slab laid down as a foundation for a building that is being constructed on soft ground

rag *noun* a roofing slate that has a rough surface on one side

rail *noun* **1.** a long horizontal or sloping piece of wood, metal or other material that is used as a barrier or support **2.** a structure made of a rail and its supports, e.g. a fence ■ *verb* to put a rail on or around something to provide a guard, barrier or support

raised access floor *noun* flooring in which the construction allows access to underfloor systems such as cabling and pipework

ramp *noun* **1.** a sloping surface that allows access from one level to a higher or lower level, or raises something up above floor or ground level **2.** a curved bend or slope in a handrail or coping where it changes direction, e.g. on a stair landing ■ *verb* to build something with a sloped surface

rampant *adjective* having a support or an abutment that is higher on one side than the other

Ramsar Site *noun* an area of wetland designated as having international importance according to the Joint Nature Conservation Committee's criteria

rate *verb* to value something, especially a property, for tax purposes

rateable value *noun* the value of a property as a basis for calculating local taxes (NOTE: The rateable value of business premises is assessed every 5 years.)

rate cap *noun* a limit on the amount an interest rate can be increased by at each adjustment period in an adjustable-rate loan. This may also include a limit on the maximum interest rate that can be charged during the life of the loan.

rate of inflation *noun* same as **inflation rate**

rates *plural noun* local tax on property

rating list *noun* a local-authority list that shows the rateable value of, and gives property descriptions of, all non-domestic properties in the area

raze *verb* to destroy or level a building or settlement completely

RCD *noun* a piece of electrical equipment, attached to a socket, that cuts the power immediately a fault is detected, to prevent injury from electric shock. Full form **residual current device**

RDA *abbreviation* Regional Development Agency

ready, willing and able purchaser agreement *noun* an agreement in which a buyer declares himself or herself to be ready, willing and able unconditionally to make a purchase of property

real *adjective* **1.** used for describing things as opposed to persons **2.** used for referring to land, especially freehold land

real burden *noun* (*in Scotland*) a form of obligation that either restricts an owner's use of his or her land, or obliges him or her to do something in relation to that land, and which benefits another piece of land in both instances

real estate *noun* land or buildings considered from a legal point of view

real estate broker *noun* same as **property broker**

real estate investment trust *noun* a property company which distributes most of its profits to shareholders, and in return qualifies for tax exemptions. Abbreviation **REIC** (NOTE: Real estate investment trusts are already in operation in the US and Australia and there is legislation underway to introduce them to the UK)

real property tax *noun US* the equivalent of council tax

realtor *noun US* an estate agent

realty *noun* property, or legal rights to land

reasonable wear and tear *noun* deterioration in the condition of property and its contents that can reasonably be considered to occur after a period of time and for which a tenant is not liable to pay compensation to a landlord at the end of the tenancy

rebuild *verb* **1.** to construct a building or other structure again because it has been damaged or destroyed **2.** to work to restore something that has been weakened, damaged or ruined **3.** to make major alterations or improvements to something

rebuilding cost *noun* the estimated cost of rebuilding a property, which is a factor in the fixing of premiums for buildings insurance

receiver *noun* someone appointed by a court to manage a business or property that is involved in a legal process such as bankruptcy

reception room *noun* a room used for entertaining guests in a house

recess *noun* a section of a wall that sits further back than the rest ■ *verb* to make a recess in a wall, or locate something in a recess

recessed lighting *noun* lighting in which the light fixture is flush or nearly flush with the wall or ceiling it is fitted into

reconnection *noun* the connecting of something again, e.g. an electricity supply that has been cut off

reconstituted stone *noun* facing blocks made of crushed natural stone bonded with synthetic substances

recyclable waste *noun* waste materials that can be recycled

recycle *verb* to process used or waste material so that it can be used again

recycled aggregates *plural noun* substances such as sand and gravel that are the by-products of industrial processes

recycling *noun* **1.** the processing of used or waste material so that it can be used again, instead of being wasted **2.** the saving or collection of used or waste material for reprocessing

redeem *verb* to pay back all the principal and interest on a loan, debt or mortgage

redemption *noun* **1.** the repayment of a loan **2.** the repayment of a debt or mortgage

redemption penalty *noun* same as **early redemption charge**

redemption statement *noun* a statement from a mortgage lender outlining the outstanding mortgage balance and how much the borrower still needs to pay in charges

redundancy insurance *noun* insurance cover that protects mortgage payments or income in the case of unexpected unemployment

reeding *noun* a set of small convex decorative mouldings on a building

re-entry *noun* the act of going back into a property

reface *verb* to restore or replace the exterior surface of a building or monument

reference *noun* a statement concerning someone's character or qualifications, usually given to a potential employer

referencing checks *plural noun* any check carried out on the history of a prospective buyer or tenant, to establish information such as payment history

refurbished *adjective* used for describing a property to which improvements to décor, fixtures and sometimes structure have been made

regeneration *noun* the redevelopment of areas that are in economic decline, in order to increase employment and stimulate new business activity

Regional Development Agency *noun* an organisation that promotes the social and economic benefits of living in a region and undertakes projects to bring new industries and jobs to the region. Abbreviation **RDA**

regional housing board *noun* a board, responsible to government, established to develop a regional housing strategy and ensure that it is implemented

regional housing strategy *noun* a regional plan to provide adequate housing for a region, drawn up by a regional housing board

regional planning body *noun* a body, responsible to government, that develops a regional spatial strategy

regional spatial strategy, regional planning policy *noun* a strategy for managing the environment of a region including areas such as housing provision, infrastructure and waste management

registered land *noun* land that has been registered with the Land Registry

registered social landlord *noun* any independent housing organisation registered with the Housing Corporation under the Housing Act 1996, often a registered charity

registered title *noun* legal evidence of a title, registered at the Land Registry

registered title deed *noun* same as **title deed**

register of charges *noun* an index of charges affecting land

register of local land charges *noun* same as **land charges register**

Register of Sasines *noun* (*in Scotland*) a record of the ownership of all heritable property in Scotland (NOTE: This has been maintained since the seventeenth century and records all deeds in relation to the ownership of heritable property in Scotland. It is being superseded by the Land Register of Scotland.)

registro catastral *noun* (*in Spain*) a tax register

registro de la propiedad *noun* (*in Spain*) the land or property register

Registry of County Court Judgments *noun* a national office that holds a register of all UK county court judgments

règlements de copropriété *noun* (*in France*) rules that govern the shared parts of a property such as an apartment block

rehab *noun* something that has been restored to good condition, especially a rehabilitated building (*informal*)

rehabilitate *verb* to restore a building, or part of a town, to its former good condition

reinstatement cost *noun* same as **rebuilding cost**

REIT *abbreviation* real estate investment trust

release fee *noun* a charge levied by your mortgage provider when moving to a new one, in return for releasing your house documents to them

relocation *noun* the act of moving house, especially to a different area or even a different country

relocation agent *noun* an agent who offers a variety of relocation services including finding suitable properties to view, raising finance and dealing with paperwork

remainder *noun* **1.** same as **residuary estate** **2.** the right to an estate that will return to the owner at the end of a lease

remainderman *noun* someone who receives the remainder of an estate

remedial work *noun* repairs to a property that a mortgage lender requires a buyer to carry out to the property before the full funds are released or within a specified period of their release

remittance *noun* **1.** the sending of money to pay for goods or services **2.** money sent as payment for goods or services

remodelling *noun* US the renovation of older properties

remortgage *verb* **1.** to revise the terms of a mortgage on a property, or to move the mortgage to a different provider **2.** to mortgage something again after the original mortgage has been paid off

removal company *noun* a company that transports the contents of one property to another property

render *verb* to cover masonry with a thin coat of plaster ■ *noun* the first thin coat of plaster applied to masonry

rendering *noun* **1.** a coat of plaster applied to masonry **2.** an architect's representation of the inside and outside of a finished building, drawn in perspective

renewable energy *noun* energy which comes from a renewable source such as solar panels or windmills, not produced by burning coal or natural gas

renewable resource *noun* **1.** a resource that can be renewed as quickly as it is used up and can, in theory, last indefinitely (NOTE: Timber, unlike mineral resources, is a renewable resource.) **2.** a source of renewable energy, e.g. sunlight, wind or waves

renewal notice *noun* a note sent by an insurance company asking the insured person to renew the insurance

renovate *verb* to bring something such as a building back to a former better state by means of repairs or redecoration

renovation *noun* the act of bringing a building back to a former better state by repairing and redecorating it

rent *noun* **1.** a regular payment made by a tenant to an owner or landlord for the right to occupy or use property **2.** a regular payment to the owner for the right to use equipment or personal property ■ *verb* **1.** to occupy someone else's property or use someone else's equipment in return for regular payments **2.** to allow someone to occupy property or use equipment in return for regular payments

Rent Act *noun* a piece of UK legislation that sets out conditions for private-sector property rental

rental *noun* **1.** money paid to occupy a property, or part of a property, for a period of time **2.** the renting of property ■ *adjective* relating to property for rent or with rent payments

rental income *noun* income from letting property (NOTE: Rental income is taxable in the UK, although different rates apply for residential (long-term) lettings and holiday lettings.)

rental market *noun* the number of people in an area who want to rent houses

rental period *noun* a period for which a property is to be rented, set out in the lease

rental price survey *noun* a survey that outlines regional average rental charges for residential properties

rental value *noun* the full value of the rent for a property if it were charged at the current market rate

rental yield *noun* the amount of money that a landlord can expect to receive in rent, expressed as a percentage of the purchase price of the property

rent a room scheme *noun* a UK government scheme in which homeowners and tenants are given tax relief on income from renting out furnished rooms in their home

rent arrears *plural noun* money owed in unpaid rent

rent assessment committee *noun* a local committee, usually comprising a solicitor, a valuer and a lay person, that fixes a rent for a property in cases where the proposed rent is disputed

rent assessment panel *noun* a regional panel from which members of rent assessment committees are drawn

rent book *noun* a book in which records are kept of rent payments made

rentcharge *noun* payment of rental on freehold land

rent controls *plural noun* government regulation of rents charged by landlords

renter *noun* 1. someone who rents property or equipment from someone else 2. someone who rents property or equipment to someone else

rent registration search *noun* a check, undertaken by a prospective tenant, for the existence of a registered fair rent level for the property in question

Rent Service *noun* a UK government agency providing a rental valuation service to local authorities in England

renunciation *noun* (*in Scotland*) an official declaration giving up a title, claim or privilege

repair *verb* to restore something broken or damaged to good condition

repair grant *noun* a local-authority grant designed to provide help towards the cost of carrying out small repairs to a property, or improving or adapting a property, awarded to people on low incomes

repairing covenant *noun* a document in which a tenant undertakes to keep the rented property in 'good and substantial repair'

repairing obligation *noun* a clause in a modern commercial lease setting out the tenant's obligations in respect of keeping the property in good order

repairs *plural noun* work carried out to make good any damage to a property or its contents

repayment method, repayment mortgage *noun* a type of mortgage repayment in which both the capital and the interest on the loan are repaid by instalments

repayment period *noun* the period over which a mortgage is repaid, usually 25 years

replacement door *noun* a new door with some heat-insulation properties, typically with a uPVC shell on an aluminium frame

replacement window *noun* a new window with some heat-insulation properties, typically with double-glazed units in a uPVC frame

repossess *verb* to take back an item that someone is buying under a hire-purchase agreement or a property that someone is buying under a mortgage because the purchaser cannot continue the repayments

repossession *noun* the act of repossessing something in a situation in which the purchaser cannot continue the mortgage repayments (NOTE: A rise in interest rates usually leads to an increase in repossessions as owners fall behind with mortgage repayments.)

resale *noun* the selling of goods that have been bought

rescind *verb* to revoke a contract and return the parties to their former positions before the contract

rescission *noun* a cancellation of a contract

reservation fee *noun* a fee charged by a lender for arranging a mortgage that is not a variable-rate mortgage

reserve fund *noun* profits in a business that have not been paid out as dividend but have been ploughed back into the business

reserve price *noun* the lowest price that a seller will accept, e.g. at an auction

residential investment *noun* a buy-to-let property

Residential Landlords Association *noun* a UK association that provides advice and support to residential landlords in the private sector

residential letting agent *noun* a letting agent who deals with residential properties

residential property *noun* houses or flats owned or occupied by individual residents

Residential Property Tribunal Service *noun* an English umbrella organisation for the five regional rent assessment panels, providing an independent tribunal service for settling disputes involving private rented and leasehold property

residential tenancy *noun* a tenancy in respect of residential property

residual current device *noun* full form of **RCD**

residuary estate *noun* **1.** the estate of a dead person that has not been bequeathed in his will **2.** what remains of an estate after the debts have been paid and bequests have been made. Also called **remainder, residue**

residuary legacy *noun* a legacy of what remains of an estate after debts, taxes and other legacies have been paid

residuary legatee *noun* someone who receives the rest of the personal property after specific legacies have been made

residue *noun* same as **residuary estate**

responsabilité civile *noun* (*in France*) third-party insurance that covers tradespeople if they accidentally damage a property in the course of renovating it

responsible lending *noun* care taken by lenders not to lend amounts that lead borrowers into excessive debt

restitution *noun* **1.** the return of property that has been illegally obtained **2.** compensation or payment for damage or loss

restitution order *noun* a court order asking for property to be returned to someone

restoration *noun* **1.** the restoring of something such as buildings or furniture to an earlier and usually better condition **2.** a building that has been brought back to an earlier and usually better condition

restriction on resale *noun* a rule that bans a buyer from reselling the property within a given period, usually enforced in cases involving overseas buyers

restrictive covenant *noun* a clause in a contract that prevents someone from doing something

resulting trust *noun* a trust that is effectively created or assumed to exist as a result of a decision by a court or of some other set of circumstances

resurface *verb* to put a new surface on something, especially a road

retail park *noun* an area in which several large retailers have outlets, typically in an out-of-town location and with car parking and other facilities provided

retail premises *plural noun* a property in which a company carries out commercial activities of some kind

retained land *noun* land owned by a company currently carrying out building work of some kind but on which the current development is not being built

retention *noun* an amount of money that is part of a sum agreed to be paid to someone but not paid until a condition has been satisfied

retirement property *noun* property designed to be occupied by retired people, typically smallish apartments in sunny overseas locations

retrospective planning application *noun* an application for planning permission that a local authority may insist a person makes who has proceeded with building work without authorisation

retrospective planning permission *noun* planning permission that is granted as a result of a retrospective planning application

return *verb* to construct part of a building such as a wall or decoration so that it turns away from its original direction ■ *noun* a profit made on an investment or business venture

reversion *noun* the return of property to an original owner when a lease expires

reversionary *adjective* used for describing property that passes to another owner on the death of the present one

reversionary interest *noun* the right to receive something in the future, e.g. on the death of a person bequeathing it

revert *verb* **1.** to return to a former state, often one perceived as inferior or less desirable **2.** to become once again the property of the former owner or his or her heirs

revetment *noun* a facing added to a structure such as a wall or building that provides additional support

revolving door *noun* a door, usually in a large building, consisting of four panels that intersect at right angles and turn on a central pivot

ribbon *noun* a strip of fabric used to tie something or for decoration

RICS *abbreviation* Royal Institution of Chartered Surveyors

ridge *noun* the line along the top of a roof where the two sloping sides meet

ridgepole *noun* a long beam of wood that runs along the ridge of a roof, supporting the upper ends of the rafters

rigger *noun* **1.** someone whose job is to erect and maintain scaffolding and lifting equipment **2.** a mechanised crane used for hoisting very large and heavy construction materials to great heights

Rightmove House Price Index *noun* a monthly housing price index compiled from asking-price data from around 150,000 UK properties

right of first refusal *noun* the right to make an offer to buy a property after other others have been submitted and with the knowledge of the value of those other offers

right of pre-emption *noun* the right to make an offer to buy property before it is offered to others

right of redemption *noun* the right to buy back property that has been lost through non-payment of debt by later paying off the debt

right of re-entry *noun* the right of a landlord to take back possession of the property if the tenant breaks his or her agreement

right of survivorship *noun* the fact that, on the death of a joint tenant, his or her rights and ownership pass to the surviving joint tenants and cannot be transferred under the terms of a will (NOTE: The right of survivorship is also called by its Latin name: *jus accrescendi*.)

right of way *noun* the right to go lawfully along a path on another person's land

Right-to-Acquire Scheme *noun* a scheme under which some tenants of social landlords have the right to buy their property

Right-to-Buy Scheme *noun* a scheme under which long-term tenants in local authority housing have the right to buy their property

right to light *noun* the right to receive a stated amount of daylight through the windows of a property, which may be infringed if, e.g., a neighbour carries out building work that creates a substantial obstruction

right-to-manage company *noun* a company that a leaseholder has requested be given the job of managing a property in place of the landlord, under the Commonhold and Leasehold Reform Act 2002

rim autobolt *noun* a lock, fitted on the surface of a door, of the type that has a latch that locks automatically when the door is closed

rim deadbolt *noun* a lock, fitted on the surface of a door, of the type that has a latch that is turned by a key

riparian rights *plural noun* the rights that apply to people who own land on the bank of a river, e.g. the right to fish in the river

riprap *noun* **1.** a stabilising foundation or embankment of loose and broken stone in or along the edge of water **2.** loose and broken stone used for riprap ■ *verb* to build or stabilise something with riprap

rise *verb* to become larger during the process of building

riser *noun* **1.** the vertical part of a step or stair **2.** a vertical pipe, duct or conduit

rising damp *noun* moisture that is absorbed from the ground into walls, resulting in structural damage. ◊ **penetrating damp**

rising main *noun* the pipe that supplies cold water from the main to a property

rivet *noun* a fastener with a head attached to a metal shaft that is passed through a hole in a material and flattened on the other side ■ *verb* **1.** to fasten something using rivets **2.** to fix or secure something firmly

rod *noun* **1.** a narrow, usually cylindrical length of wood, metal, plastic or other material **2.** a graduated pole used by surveyors for sighting with a levelling instrument to determine elevation differences **3.** a board on which the dimensions of a joinery assembly such as a window or door frame are marked in full scale

rogito *noun* (*in Italy*) a deed of purchase

rolled steel joist *noun* a steel beam used for structural support, e.g. to support the weight of an upper wall when a doorway is knocked through a lower wall. Abbreviation **RSJ**

roller *noun* a painting tool in the form of a revolving tube with a soft absorbent covering and a handle, used for applying paint to large surface areas

roller blind *noun* a window blind which is raised by winding it onto a roller above the window

Roman blind *noun* a window blind consisting of slatted wood or fabric which is raised using a cord

rone *noun Scottish* **1.** a gutter at the edge of a roof, for channelling rain away **2.** a drainpipe that channels rainwater down the side of a building away from a roof gutter

roof *noun* the outside covering of the top of a building, or the framework supporting this ■ *verb* to fix a roof onto a building

roof hatch *noun* a hatch in a ceiling that leads into an area of roof space

roofing *noun* **1.** material used to make a roof **2.** the business or occupation of making or repairing roofs

roof insulation *noun* any of various materials designed to be fitted to the inner or outer surface of a pitched roof to provide heat insulation

rooflight *noun* a small window set into a roof

roof space *noun* the space between the inner surface of a roof and the ceiling of an upper room, especially when not floored to produce a loft or attic

roof tile *noun* any of various modular surfacing materials for roofs that are not slates, typically made of baked clay

roof truss *noun* a set of timbers that form a section of the structure of a pitched roof, typically prefabricated

roof valley *noun* a valley between two pitched sections of a large roof

room *noun* an area within a building that is enclosed by a floor, walls and a ceiling

root of title *noun* the basic title deed that proves that a vendor has the right to sell a property

rose *noun* **1.** a circular fitting on a ceiling through which the lead of an electric light passes **2.** same as **rose window**

rose window, rose *noun* a round window with central piece of stone that has stone spokes radiating from it

rotunda *noun* **1.** a round building, usually covered with a dome **2.** a large round hall or room

roughcast *noun* a surface of coarse plaster covered with pebbles on the outside walls of a building ■ *verb* to cover the surface of a wall, or the walls of a building, with roughcast

rough-hewn, rough-cut *adjective* of masonry work, cut or shaped only roughly, with the surface and the edges not smoothed

rout *verb* to cut a groove in wood or metal, especially with a router cutter

router cutter *noun* a machine or tool that cuts a groove in wood

Royal Incorporation of Architects Scotland *noun* the professional body for all chartered architects in Scotland and the foremost architectural professional institute in the country

Royal Institute of British Architects *noun* the foremost professional body for architects in the UK, whose aim is to advance architecture by demonstrating benefit to society and promoting excellence in the profession

Royal Institution of Chartered Surveyors *noun* the foremost UK body for professionals involved in land, property, construction and environmental issues. Abbreviation **RICS**

Royal Institution of Chartered Surveyors Housing Market Survey *noun* a monthly survey of UK house prices published by the Royal Institution of Chartered Surveyors

Royal Society of Architects in Wales *noun* the foremost professional body for architects in Wales

Royal Town Planning Institute *noun* a UK body that promotes good planning and seeks to influence government policy affecting the built environment

RSJ *abbreviation* rolled steel joist

rubble *noun* **1.** broken stones, bricks and other materials from buildings that have fallen down or been demolished **2.** rough unfinished stones used to fill space between walls or to build the bulk of a wall that will have a finishing surface of dressed stone **3.** masonry that is constructed using rough unfinished stones

run off *noun* rainfall that does not soak into the soil but flows into surface waters

ruoli *noun* (*in Italy*) a register of licensed estate agents

rural development area *noun* a rural area identified as having a concentration of economic and social needs, and where rural regeneration activities are focused

rural exception site *noun* a rural area that has been largely ignored in schemes to create affordable housing for people on low incomes

rural exceptions policy *noun* a policy to create affordable housing in rural exception sites

rural home ownership grant *noun* (*in Scotland*) a scheme to assist households on low to medium incomes in rural areas to build or acquire their own home

rustic *adjective* **1.** relating to, characteristic of or appropriate to the country or country living **2.** with a rough finish ■ *noun* brick or stone with a rough finish. Also called **rusticwork**

rusticate *verb* to finish the outside of a wall with large blocks of masonry that are left with a rough surface, are bevelled, and have deep joints between them

rustication *noun* surfaces of stonework left deliberately rough or deliberately roughened, to create a rustic effect

rusticwork *noun* same as **rustic**

S

safe home income plan *noun* a scheme that guarantees that homeowners releasing equity in a home reversion scheme will have rent-free tenure and will not become victims of negative equity

safety certificate *noun* a document certifying that all electrical and gas appliances and systems in a property have been tested and found to be safe

safety gate *noun* a gate fitted, e.g. at the foot or head of a staircase, to prevent toddlers and young children from entering a potentially dangerous area of a property

safety inspection *noun* an inspection of property rented from a private landlord undertaken to assess whether it is safe to live in, conducted by a local authority official

sale *noun* the act of selling or transferring an item or a property from one owner to another in exchange for money

sale and lease-back *noun* a situation in which a company sells a property to raise cash and then leases it back from the purchaser

sale by auction *noun* a sale of property in which prospective buyers bid at an auction

sale by tender *noun* a sale of property in which prospective buyers submit offers, as distinct from a sale by auction

sale of part *noun* a sale of a part of a property only, not of the complete property

sales particulars *plural noun* details of a property for sale, provided by an estate agent

sales tax *noun US* same as **VAT**

salvage *verb* to save used, damaged or rejected goods for recycling or further use

sand *noun* a substance consisting of fine loose grains of rock or minerals, usually quartz fragments, found on beaches, in deserts and in soil, widely used as a building material ■ *verb* **1.** to rub a surface with glasspaper to make it smoother **2.** to add sand to something, e.g. to a mixture of materials when making mortar

sandbag *noun* a sealed bag full of sand, used in building defences against flooding

sander *noun* an electric power tool that is used to smooth wooden or metal surfaces

sanitaryware *noun* fixtures such as toilets, bidets and basins

SAP *abbreviation* Standard Assessment Procedure

SAP calculations *plural noun* calculations done in order to arrive at the carbon dioxide emission rate of a property, according to Standard Assessment Procedure standards

sarking board *noun* wooden boards used for forming the surface of a pitched roof, to which roofing felt and slates or tiles are fixed

sash *noun* a frame holding the glass panes of a window or door

sash stop *noun* a catch fitted to the frame of a sash window to control the extent to which it can open

sash window *noun* a window that consists of two frames, one above the other in vertical grooves, allowing either to be opened or shut by sliding it up or down

Sasine Register *noun* same as **General Register of Sasines**

saw doctor *noun* a machine that gives a saw a serrated edge

sawyer *noun* someone who saws wood for a living

scabbler *noun* a tool or machine used for giving a rough keyed surface to concrete on which further construction is to take place

scaffold *noun* a temporary framework of poles and planks that is used to support workers and materials during the erection, repair or decoration of a building ■ *verb* to put up a scaffold around or against a building

scaffolder *noun* a contractor who erects scaffolding

scaffolding *noun* **1.** a scaffold or system of scaffolds around or against a building **2.** the poles and planks used to build a scaffold

scantling *noun* **1.** a piece of timber with a small cross section, e.g. a rafter **2.** the dimension of a building material

scarf *noun* **1.** a joint made by joining two notched boards together. Also called **scarf joint 2.** either of the notched ends of a scarf ■ *verb* to join boards together by means of a scarf

schedule *noun* a list of details, often in the form of an appendix to a legal or legislative document

scheduled ancient monument *noun* a protected archaeological site or historic building considered to be of national importance

ScotLIS *abbreviation* Scottish Land Information Service

Scottish Building Employers Federation *noun* the premier employer's federation representing the building industry in Scotland

Scottish Civic Trust *noun* a voluntary organisation working to raise the quality of the whole built environment in Scotland

Scottish Environmental Protection Agency *noun* Scotland's environmental regulator and adviser, responsible to the Scottish parliament through ministers, working to control pollution and protect and improve the environment

Scottish Land Information Service *noun* a service that gives access to a wide range of computer-based information about land in Scotland. Abbreviation **ScotLIS**

Scottish Legal Services Ombudsman *noun* (*in Scotland*) an official who investigates complaints about the way in which a professional body has handled a complaint against a legal practitioner

Scottish Property Network *noun* (*in Scotland*) a joint venture between Scottish Enterprise and the University of Paisley that aims to provide up-to-date information on market activity in Scottish industrial and commercial property markets

Scottish Solicitors' Discipline Tribunal *noun* (*in Scotland*) an independent body that mainly deals with serious disciplinary issues that arise within the legal profession

Scottish Water *noun* a publicly owned business responsible for the public water supply in Scotland, answerable to the Scottish parliament

scratch coat *noun* a first coat of plaster

screed *noun* **1.** a strip of plaster, wood or other material placed on a surface as a guide to the correct thickness of plaster or concrete to be applied there **2.** a board or tool used to level a layer of concrete, sand or other loose material **3.** a smooth top layer on a concrete floor or other surface

screeded floor *noun* a floor of solid cement, with or without trunking incorporated for cables and pipes

screeding timber *noun* a straight-edged piece of timber used for making wet concrete level on a screeded floor

screed rail *noun* a temporary or permanent edging for a screeded floor

screen *noun* **1.** a fixed or movable partition or frame that is used to conceal, divide, separate or provide shelter **2.** a decorative frame or partition, e.g. in a church choir

screw *noun* **1.** a piece of metal with a tapering threaded body and grooved head by which it is turned into something in order to fasten things together **2.** a screw with a blunt end onto which a nut is fitted to hold two objects together

scrim *noun* a durable open-weave cotton or linen fabric used as a lining material in upholstery

seal *noun* a tight closure that prevents a substance such as air or water from entering or escaping

sealant *noun* a substance used to seal something, e.g. by filling gaps or making a surface nonporous

sealed bid, sealed offer *noun* (*in Scotland*) an offer to purchase property, submitted in a sealed envelope at a closing date

sealing *noun* the act of repaying a mortgage in full by making the final mortgage payment and any other outstanding charges

sealing fee *noun* same as **release fee**

searches *plural noun* examinations of registers and records to determine any encumbrances affecting the title to property

second charge *noun* same as **secured loan**

second home *noun* a second property owned by somebody which they use as a personal residence and not as a source of rental income

second mortgage *noun* a further mortgage on a property that is already mortgaged. The first mortgage has prior claim.

secured creditor *noun* a person who is owed money by someone and holds a mortgage or charge on that person's property as security

secured loan *noun* a loan that is guaranteed by the borrower giving valuable property as security

secure tenant *noun* a tenant of a local authority who has the right to buy the freehold of the property he or she rents at a discount

security *noun* something pledged to guarantee fulfilment of an obligation, especially an asset guaranteeing repayment of a loan that becomes the property of the creditor if the loan is not repaid

security of tenure *noun* the right to keep rented accommodation, provided that conditions are met

seisin *noun* **1.** the legal freehold possession of land **2.** the act of taking legal freehold possession of land **3.** land that is wholly and legally owned, especially land taken possession of legally

self-build *noun* the building of a home in which the homeowner organises the project independently, from design to construction, as distinct from simply buying a ready-made home from a developer

self-build mortgage *noun* a mortgage provided to finance a self-build

self-certification mortgage *noun* a mortgage for which no proof of income is required

self storage *noun* a property divided into storage units of varying sizes that are rented to people who store their personal property there

sell *verb* to offer a particular property for sale

seller *noun* a person or company that offers a property for sale

seller's market *noun* a market in which the seller can ask high prices because there is a large demand for the product. Opposite **buyer's market**

selling price *noun* the price at which someone is willing to sell a property or service

semi-detached *adjective* joined to a neighbouring building by a shared wall ■ *noun* a house with a wall in common with the next house

separación de bienes *noun* (*in Spain*) the separate ownership of assets, including property, within a marriage

separate property *noun* property owned by a husband and wife before their marriage. ◊ **community property**

séparation de biens *noun* (*in France*) the separate ownership of assets, including property, within a marriage

separator *noun* a device that removes a component from a mixture or combination

sequestration *noun* the taking and keeping of property on the order of a court, especially seizing property from someone who is in contempt of court

sequestrator *noun* someone who takes and keeps property on the order of a court

service charge *noun* a sum of money charged to leasehold owners of flats for the maintenance of communal areas such as halls, lifts and gardens

servient owner *noun* the owner of land over which someone else (the dominant owner) has a right to use a path

servient tenement *noun* (*in Scotland*) land or property over which a neighbouring property (the **dominant tenement**) has a right or easement

servitude *noun* (*in Scotland*) a restriction or obligation attached to a property that entitles someone other than the owner to a specific use of it, e.g. the right to cross it

settle *verb* 1. to reach a settlement 2. to write something such as a contract out in its final form

settled land *noun* land that is subject of a settlement in a will

settlement *noun* 1. a restriction in a will that ensures that property stays in the ownership of the family of the deceased, or ensures that the property is held in trust for the deceased's family and that they receive any income from the sale of it 2. an agreement reached after discussion or negotiation 3. an agreement reached without completing legal proceedings 4. the payment of a bill, debt or claim 5. subsidence in a building 6. a conveyance of property to someone or to the trustees for someone 7. a document recording a conveyance of property

settlement day *noun* in Scottish conveyancing, the date when the solicitors for the two parties meet, when the purchaser pays and the vendor passes the conveyance and the deeds to the purchaser

settlor *noun* someone who settles property on someone

se vende *phrase* (*in Spain*) 'for sale'

several tenancy *noun* the holding of property by a number of people, each separately and not jointly with any other person

sewer *noun* a large pipe or tunnel that takes urine and faeces away from buildings

sewerage *noun* 1. a system of sewers 2. the removal of sewage by means of sewers

shared equity *noun* a house-purchasing scheme in which an individual buyer shares the cost and the ownership with a local authority

shared freehold *noun* a situation in which a freehold is shared by two or more individuals from separate households

shared garden *noun* a garden that is shared by two or more households

shared tenancy *noun* a situation in which a tenancy is shared by two or more individuals from separate households

share of freehold *noun* a share of the freehold of a multi-occupancy property obtained by owners of leasehold flats in the property

share-to-buy mortgage *noun* a type of mortgage which allows 2 or more friends to buy a property together, giving joint ownership

Sharia-compliant mortgage *noun* same as **Islamic mortgage**

shell *noun* the basic framework of a building, especially while under construction or after damage by fire

Shelter *noun* a UK charity working to eradicate bad housing and homelessness

sheriff *noun* (*in Scotland*) a judge who presides over a sheriff court, one of the lower courts for civil and criminal cases

sheriff officer *noun* (*in Scotland*) a legal officer who serves under a sheriff and is empowered to take possession of a debtor's property, forcibly if necessary, to serve writs and to make arrests (NOTE: In the rest of the UK, these duties are undertaken by a *bailiff*.)

shingle *noun* a small flat tile, especially one made of wood, used in overlapping rows to cover a roof or wall ■ *verb* to cover something with small overlapping tiles

SHIP *abbreviation* safe home income plan

short assured tenancy *noun Scottish* same as **assured shorthold tenancy**

shortfall *noun* an amount that is missing from a total expected or required sum

shortfall debt *noun* debt arising when an endowment fails to yield enough money to pay off a mortgage

shorthold agreement *noun* a tenancy agreement for a short period, often less than a year

shorthold tenancy *noun* a protected tenancy for a limited period of less than five years

shorthold tenant *noun* a tenant on a shorthold agreement

short-term let *noun* a letting of property for a short term only, usually less than a year

shower *noun* **1.** a device that sprays water downwards for people to stand under and wash **2.** an enclosure in which a shower is fitted

shower screen *noun* a rigid screen over a bath, fitted to contain the spray from a shower fitted over the bath

show house *noun* a house or flat that is built and furnished so that potential buyers can see what similar houses could be like

shrinkage *noun* a reduction in size of some construction materials as they dry out, which can cause structural instability

shrinkage crack *noun* a crack that can occur in concrete structures as they dry out

shroud *noun* a protective covering, e.g. a guard for a piece of machinery

shutter *noun* a hinged external cover for a door or window, often with louvres and usually fitted in pairs ▪ *verb* to close or protect something by means of shutters

sill *noun* the horizontal ledge at the bottom of a window or door frame. Also called **cill**

single bedroom *noun* a bedroom that is large enough for a single bed but not for a double bed, or a bedroom that has a single bed in it

single-tier lease *noun* a lease for a flat in a property converted into flats

sink *noun* a basin that is fixed or mounted against a wall, and has a piped water supply and drainage ▪ *verb* **1.** to descend, or appear to descend, from a higher position or level to a lower one **2.** to fall or collapse slowly **3.** to drill a well, tunnel or shaft in the ground **4.** to invest or lose money in a business or project

sinking fund *noun* a fund built up out of amounts of money put aside regularly to meet a future need

sink waste *noun* waste water and other substances that flows from a kitchen sink

site *noun* an area or piece of land where something was, is or will be located

site inspection *noun* an inspection to monitor the quality of workmanship and materials used in a construction project. Also called **site visit**

site insurance *noun* insurance that gives protection against a wide spread of risks on a self-build project, evidence of which is often required by a lender

site manager *noun* a person who oversees the way a major construction site is organised and managed

Site of Nature Conservation Importance *noun* an area regarded by a local authority as worthy of conservation but not operating as a local nature reserve

site visit *noun* same as **site inspection**

skeleton key *noun* a key that will fit several different doors in a building

skim *verb* to coat a wall with a thin layer of plaster

skip *noun* a large flat-bottomed metal container kept outdoors for putting unwanted materials, furniture or any bulky refuse in, especially when a building is being renovated or constructed

skip permit *noun* a permit granted by a local authority that allows a skip to be kept on a public road temporarily

skirting board, skirting *noun* a narrow board, attached to the base of an interior wall, that covers the joint between the wall and the floor

skyline *noun* the pattern of shapes made by the various features of a landscape, e.g. hills or buildings, against the sky

slab *noun* **1.** a thick flat broad piece of something, especially when cut or trimmed **2.** a flat rectangular base or foundation of concrete or stone

slabbing *noun* **1.** the laying of stone or concrete slabs to form a surface such as a pathway **2.** stone or concrete slabs, collectively

sleeper *noun* a heavy beam used as a sill, footing or support

slippage *noun* the movement of land resulting from natural shifts or human activity, frequently causing structural damage to buildings

slush *verb* to fill masonry joints with mortar, or cover a surface with cement

small print *noun* information printed at the end of a contract or other official document in smaller letters than the rest of the text, often containing important details that might be overlooked

smoke alarm *noun* a device intended to give a warning of fire by triggering an alarm when it detects the presence of smoke

snagging list *noun* a list of faults that the purchaser of a new property compiles and passes on to the builder to address

snagging survey *noun* a survey of a new property carried out on behalf of the homeowner for the purpose of identifying faults for the builder to address

soakaway *noun* a channel in the ground filled with gravel, designed to take rainwater from a downpipe or liquid sewage from a septic tank and into surrounding soil where it can be absorbed

social HomeBuy *noun* a government scheme designed to allow social housing tenants to buy their current home either outright or on shared ownership terms, usually in partnership with the landlord, with the benefit of a discount

social housing *noun* housing provided by organisations such as local authorities or housing associations for renting at lower than market rates to people who cannot afford to buy their own homes or rent privately

social landlord *noun* same as **housing association**

Society for the Protection of Ancient Buildings *noun* a campaigning and educating organisation established to protect old buildings from decay, demolition and damage

socket *noun* **1.** a hole or recess in something specially shaped to receive a specific object or part, e.g. the hole that receives a light bulb **2.** a receptacle, usually mounted on a wall, into which an electric plug is inserted to make a connection to a source of electric power

soft landscaping *noun* plants and other natural features of a designed landscape, as distinct from walls, fences and other structures

soil investigation *noun* same as **ground investigation**

soil pipe *noun* a pipe through which toilet waste flows from the pan to the soil stack

soil stack *noun* a large-bore external pipe that takes toilet waste from a soil pipe into a sewer

solar gain *noun* the amount of heat in a building derived from solar radiation through windows or transparent walls

solar heating *noun* the use of the Sun's energy to heat water as it passes through heat-absorbing panels

solar panel *noun* a large panel containing light- or heat-absorbing plates that convert the sun's radiation into renewable energy for use in the home

sold subject to contract *phrase* used for describing the status of a property on which an offer to purchase has been accepted by the seller but for which contracts have not yet been exchanged

sold subject to survey *phrase* used for describing the status of a property on which an offer to purchase has been made subject to the satisfactory completion of a survey on the property, usually carried out at the buyer's expense

sole agency *noun* an agreement that only one particular estate agent has the right to look for buyers for your property

sole occupancy *noun* the occupying of a property by a single individual, which attracts a discount on council tax payments

soleplate *noun* the plate that supports the bases of the studs used in framing a wall

sole selling rights *plural noun* the right of an appointed estate agent to be paid commission on the sale of the property even if he or she does nothing to bring about the sale

solicitor *noun* a lawyer who gives legal advice, draws up legal documents, and does preparatory work for barristers

solicitors' charges *plural noun* payments to be made to solicitors for work done on behalf of clients

solum *noun* (*in Scotland*) the ground on which property has been built

sound level meter *noun* a piece of electrical equipment used to measure the level of noise in an area, used, e.g., in investigations of claims for noise pollution

soundproofing *noun* methods and materials used to reduce the noise emitted from a property or entering a property from outside sources

spacer block *noun* a block used for holding apart the panes of glass that form a sealed unit in a double-glazed window or door

Spacia *noun* a company that is the UK's largest small business landlord

spanner *noun* a hand tool with fixed or movable jaws, used for turning nuts and bolts

spec *noun* same as **specification**

special conditions of sale *plural noun* conditions imposed by lenders in relation to a property being sold at auction

special indorsement *noun* full details of a claim involving money, land or goods that a claimant is trying to recover

specialist report *noun* a report prepared by a specialist surveyor or company investigating a particular aspect of a property, e.g. the system of electrical wiring, central heating or roofing

specialist test equipment *noun* equipment used by specialists carrying out surveys on particular aspects of a property, e.g. dampness levels in the walls

specialist waste *noun* waste that must be disposed of using services other than a local authority's standard refuse collection service

special needs housing *noun* residential properties adapted for use by people with special needs

special protection area *noun* an area that is the home of, or is visited by, wild birds that are subject to special conservation measures (NOTE: Property in a Special Conservation Area may be subject to stricter than usual planning permission regulations, to avoid work which would disturb the birds.)

special rate period *noun* a period during the term of a mortgage within which a lower interest rate applies

specification *noun* a detailed description, especially one providing information needed to make, build or produce something

specific devise *noun* a gift of a specified property to someone in a will

spigot *noun* the end of a pipe that is joined by insertion into the enlarged end of another pipe

spike *noun* **1.** a sharply pointed piece of metal or wood, especially one of a number along the top of a railing, fence or wall **2.** a long heavy metal nail

spile *noun* a heavy timber post driven into the ground as a foundation or support

spill *noun* a small plug used to stop up a hole

spindle *noun* **1.** a long thin piece of wood that is shaped somewhat like the spindle of a spinning wheel, e.g. a baluster **2.** a rotating rod on a device such as a door handle

spirit level *noun* a tool used for checking the horizontal or vertical alignment of something, typically with a tube containing liquid with a bubble in it, the position of the bubble being the indicator of alignment

spray paint *noun* paint applied under pressure from an aerosol can or spray gun

sprig *noun* a small headless tack that tapers to a point

sprinkler *noun* a device that sends out a moving spray of water, used for watering gardens or for suppressing fires

sprinkler detection system *noun* a fire detection system which, when activated by smoke or flames, immediately sprays water on the fire

squat *verb* to occupy land or buildings without permission of the owner or other rights holder ■ *noun* a piece of property that is occupied by squatters

squatter *noun* someone who squats in someone else's property

squatter's rights *plural noun* rights of a person who is squatting in another person's property to remain in unlawful possession of premises until ordered to leave by a court

stabilised rate mortgage *noun* a mortgage in which a nominal rate is set that is designed to reflect the likely average rate over a period, but the rate charged to the account may vary in line with market conditions

stage payments *noun* a method of payment on a self-build project, in which the buyer makes payments to the builder/developer in stages

staging *noun* a temporary structure of supports and platforms used while people are building or working on something

stain block paint *noun* paint applied over stains and marks on walls to seal them before a further coat of emulsion is applied

stairs *plural noun* a set or several sets of steps leading from one floor or level to another

stairwell *noun* the vertical space in a building where stairs are located

stakeholder *noun* a person or group with a direct interest, involvement or investment in something, e.g. shareholders in a property investment scheme

stamp duty *noun* a tax on documents recording legal activities such as the conveyance of a property to a new owner or the contract for the purchase of shares

stamp duty exempt area *noun* an area regarded as disadvantaged and in which the purchase and sale of properties is exempt from stamp duty

stamp duty land tax *noun* a form of tax payable on the purchase and sale of land

stamp duty land tax certificate *noun* a certificate issued when stamp duty land tax has been paid

stamp duty land tax disadvantaged area *noun* an area regarded as disadvantaged and in which transactions relating to land attract discounts on stamp duty land tax

stamp duty land tax disadvantaged area search *noun* a check, carried out by a conveyancer on behalf of a prospective buyer, to ascertain whether the property is situated within a stamp duty land tax disadvantaged area

Stamp Duty (Disadvantaged Areas) Regulations *plural noun* UK legislation which sets out the standards for identifying stamp duty exempt areas

Standard Assessment Procedure *noun* the UK government's scheme for assessing the energy rating of properties. Abbreviation **SAP**

standard construction *noun* a property the design and construction of which is regarded as standard, especially by a lender offering a mortgage on the property

standard mortgage *noun* a mortgage of the type usually offered by high-street lenders, offering a range of interest rates and payment options

standard variable rate *noun* an interest rate on mortgage payments that varies as the Bank of England's base rate varies

staple *noun* a small U-shaped piece of strong metal wire with two sharp points, usually driven into a surface to hold something such as a bolt or cable in place

Starter Home Initiative *noun* same as **key worker living programme**

statement of community involvement *noun* a local authority document designed to show how the council intends to engage the community on all major planning applications

statute of limitations *noun* a law that allows only a certain amount of time, usually six years, for someone to start legal proceedings to claim something, e.g. property or compensation for damage

statutory *adjective* **1.** regulated or imposed by statute **2.** covered by a statute, and subject to the penalty laid down by that statute

statutory body *noun* an organisation with the legal authority to take action in respect of a particular area of life

statutory declaration *noun* **1.** an official signed statement which is legally binding, such as one made during the sale of a property **2.** a declaration signed and witnessed for official purposes

statutory nuisance *noun* a nuisance on a list of those to which abatement procedures apply, under the Environmental Protection Act, including smoke emission, the keeping of animals and noise pollution

statutory periodic tenancy *noun* a situation in which a fixed-term tenancy has ended and no new agreement has been signed for a new fixed-term tenancy

steel reinforced concrete *noun* concrete inside which a steel mesh or lattice creates reinforcement

stepped rate *noun* an interest rate that increases in steps, usually yearly, to a particular fixed rate, designed to keep interest payments low in the early years

stepped rate mortgage *noun* a mortgage that offers a stepped rate

stereobate *noun* **1.** a masonry platform that supports a building **2.** same as **stylobate**

sterling board *noun* a construction material made from softwood strands compressed and glued together with exterior grade, water-resistant resins, used where the appearance of the surface is unimportant, e.g. as sarking

stilt *noun* a tall post or column that supports a structure above land or water

stilted *adjective* used for describing an arch that is joined to the top part of the pillar, column or wall supporting it by vertical pieces of stone

stipple *noun* a rough grainy finish in wet paint or plaster, produced by means of dabbing strokes

stock brick *noun* a type of traditional-looking brick with a slightly irregular shape made by using a mechanised moulding process

stone *noun* **1.** the hard solid nonmetallic substance that rocks are made of, widely used as a building material **2.** a piece of rock that has been shaped for a particular purpose, e.g. a paving stone

stone cladding *noun* a layer of stone with a distinctive finish, added to the outside of a building to improve its appearance

stone-faced *adjective* having a facing of stone

stonework *noun* **1.** the parts of a building or other structure that are made of stone **2.** the process of building with stone

stop bead *noun* a metal trim that reinforces the edge of a thin plaster coating on a wall

stopcock *noun* a valve or tap used to turn on or turn off a house's supply of water

storage *noun* space in which to store things, especially the amount of such space

storm drain *noun* a specially wide channel for taking away large amounts of rainwater that fall during heavy storms

stretcher *noun* **1.** a strong, usually horizontal beam or bar that is used as a brace in the framework of a structure **2.** a brick or stone laid in a wall so that its longer edge forms part of the face of the wall. Compare **header**

stretcher bond *noun* a style of bricklaying in which every course of bricks has the bricks laid side on, with no courses laid end on

stringer *noun* a heavy horizontal timber used for structural purposes

strip *verb* **1.** to remove old paint or varnish from a surface by scraping or burning it or by using a chemical **2.** to remove all the contents from a room or building

strip lighting *noun* same as **fluorescent lighting**

stripper *noun* a tool or substance used for removing paint, varnish, wallpaper or other substances from a surface

structural *adjective* **1.** relating to the way parts are put together or how they work together **2.** suitable for use in construction **3.** constituting an important or essential part of a structure

structural engineer *noun* an engineer who advises on the design of a building project and the choice of structural materials used, and who often carries out safety inspections during the course of the project

structural engineering *noun* a person who decides how new constructions should be built, using which materials, so that they are durable and safe to live in

structural survey *noun* same as **full structural survey**

structure *noun* a building, bridge, framework or other large object that has been put together from many different parts

strut *noun* a long rigid plank, board or other structural member used as a support in building ■ *verb* to support a structure with planks or boards

stucco *noun* **1.** plaster used for surfacing interior or exterior walls, often used in association with classical mouldings **2.** decorative work moulded from stucco. Also called **stuccowork** ■ *verb* to apply a coating of stucco to a wall

stud *noun* **1.** a small metal knob, rivet or nail head that protrudes slightly from a surface, especially for decorative effect **2.** a vertical length of timber to which material such as lath or plasterboard is attached in constructing a wall **3.** a headless bolt that is smooth in the centre and threaded at each end

stud detector *noun* a piece of electrical equipment that locates wooden frames, live wires and metal pipes in stud walls

student let *noun* a letting of property to students

stud wall *noun* an internal wall consisting of a wooden frame with a plasterboard surface

study *noun* a room used for work that involves reading, thinking or writing

stylobate *noun* a continuous raised platform of masonry supporting a row of columns. Also called **stereobate**

subbase *noun* **1.** a deep layer of large stones that forms the lowest level of a roadbed or of the foundation of a building **2.** the lowest section of any base or foundation, e.g. the bottom part of a pedestal

subcontract *noun* a secondary contract in which the person or company originally hired to do a job in turn hires somebody else to do all or part of the work ■ *verb* to pass on work to a second person or company under the terms of a subcontract

subcontractor *noun* a company that has a contract to do work for a main contractor

subdivide *verb* to divide a section, or all the sections, of something into sections that are smaller still

subdivision *noun* the act of dividing a property in two or more parts into units that are smaller still

subject to contract *phrase* ♦ **sold subject to contract**

subject to survey *noun* ♦ **sold subject to survey**

sublease *verb* to lease a leased property from another tenant

sublessee *noun* a person or company that holds a property on a sublease

sublessor *noun* a tenant who lets a leased property to another tenant

sublet *verb* to let a leased property to another tenant

subsidence *noun* the sinking down of land resulting from natural shifts or human activity, frequently causing structural damage to buildings

substantial interference *noun* any action legally regarded as constituting a major breach of the rights of another individual

substructure *noun* the foundation of an erected structure

subtenancy *noun* an agreement to sublet a property

subtenant *noun* a person or company to which a property has been sublet

suburb *noun* a residential part of a town, away from the centre, but still within the built-up area

suburban *adjective* relating to, belonging to or located in a suburb

succession *noun* the act of acquiring a property or title from someone who has died

sum assured *noun* the minimum amount of money that is guaranteed to be paid at the term of an endowment policy

summary valuation *noun* a document that explains how the rateable value of a business property has been calculated

summer *noun* **1.** a principal horizontal beam in a building used to support floor joists. Also called **summertree 2.** a stone that lies on top of a pier, column or wall and supports one or more arches **3.** same as **lintel**

sun deck *noun* a balcony, terrace or platform attached to a building, used for sunbathing

superstructure *noun* the part of a building above its foundations

surface *noun* **1.** a solid flat area, e.g. the area on top of kitchen cabinets **2.** a relatively thin outer layer or coating applied to something, usually to give it a smooth finish

surface mounted lock *noun* any lock of a type mounted on the rim of a door, as distinct from a mortice lock

surface water *noun* water that flows across the surface of the soil as a stream after rain and drains into rivers rather than seeping into the soil itself

surfacing *noun* materials used to create the surface of roads and footpaths

surrender *noun* the abandonment of legal rights, especially the giving up of a lease or an insurance policy before it has expired

surrender value *noun* money that an insurer will pay if an insurance policy is given up before it matures

survey *noun* **1.** an inspection of a building to determine its condition and assess its value **2.** a report that results from inspecting the condition and assessing the value of a building **3.** an act of taking detailed measurements of an area of land **4.** a report that shows the results of a survey undertaken to measure an area of land ∎ *verb* **1.** to inspect a building in order to determine its structural soundness or assess its value **2.** to make a detailed map of an area of land, including its boundaries, area and elevation, using geometry and trigonometry to measure angles and distances

survey fee *noun* a fee charged for the service of providing a surveyor's report

surveyor *noun* **1.** someone whose occupation is inspecting buildings to determine the soundness of their construction or to assess their value **2.** someone whose occupation is taking accurate measurements of land areas in order to determine boundaries, elevations and dimensions **3.** same as **quantity surveyor**

Surveyor Ombudsman Scheme *noun* (*in Scotland*) a scheme to investigate consumer complaints by residential owners and tenants against chartered surveyors working on property

Surveyors' and Valuers' Association *noun* a national accreditation body for UK surveyors and valuers

Surveyors' Arbitration Scheme *noun* a scheme to investigate complaints by residential owners against chartered surveyors in the UK

survivorship *noun* the state of being the survivor of two or more people who hold a joint tenancy on a property

suspended ceiling *noun* a layer of tiles which is held on wires slightly below the level of the permanent ceiling, used to give a smooth appearance where there are uneven joists

suspended timber floor *noun* a wooden floor supported from beneath by joists

switchboard *noun* one or more insulating panels containing the electrical devices and instruments, e.g. switches, circuit breakers, fuses and meters, required to operate electrical equipment

synchronisation of contracts *noun* in a property chain, the practice of ensuring that exchanges of contracts relating to the various properties in the chain take place at roughly the same time, to ensure a smooth handover of properties

synthetic fibre *noun* any fibre made from synthetic materials such as nylon, acrylic and polypropylene

T

tacit relocation *noun* (*in Scotland*) implied consent to the renewal of a lease if notice is not given in good time

tack *noun* a small sharp nail with a broad head

tail *verb* to build one end of something such as a joist, beam or brick into a wall, or be fixed into a wall at one end

tailpiece *noun* a beam that has one end embedded in a wall

tallboy *noun* **1.** a high piece of furniture, typically comprising two chests of drawers set one on top of the other or a chest of drawers with a cupboard or hanging space above **2.** a narrow fitting at the top of a chimney to prevent smoke being carried back down

tangible assets *plural noun* assets that are visible, e.g. machinery, buildings, furniture or jewellery. Compare **intangible assets**

tarmac a trade name for a material used for surfacing roads

tarpaulin *noun* **1.** a heavy waterproof material, especially treated canvas, used as a covering and to protect things from moisture **2.** a sheet of tarpaulin

taxe foncière *noun* (*in France*) a land tax payable whether or not anyone is living in a property

taxe sur la valeur *noun* (*in France*) the equivalent of VAT. Abbreviation **TVA**

tax inspector *noun* an official of the Inland Revenue who examines tax returns and decides how much tax someone should pay

tax office *noun* a local office of the Inland Revenue

tax return *noun* the set of government forms on which earnings and expenses are recorded in order to calculate the tax liability of a person or business

TDSRA *abbreviation* Tenancy Deposit Scheme for Regulated Agents

technical services department *noun* the department of a local authority that deals with planning and building control

Telecommunications Industry Association *noun* a UK association providing support and representation for contractors and companies engaged in telecommunications business

telemeter *noun* any measuring device that uses radiowaves or microwaves

television aerial *noun* a device for receiving broadcast television signals, typically mounted on a roof

temper *noun* the degree of hardness of a metal ■ *verb* **1.** to make glass stronger and liable to shatter when broken, to prevent major injuries, either by heating it or by the use of chemicals **2.** to harden metal by heating it to very high temperatures and then cooling it

tempered glass *noun* toughened glass designed to shatter when struck and so prevent major injuries, used for such items as entrance doors and shower screens

template *noun* a short beam of metal, wood, or stone used to distribute weight or pressure in a structure

temporary rented accommodation *noun* temporary accommodation in a rental property that is not a permanent home, e.g. for someone waiting for a purchased property to become available or for someone working part of the week in another town

tenancy *noun* **1.** an agreement by which a person can occupy a property **2.** the period during which a person has an agreement to occupy a property

tenancy at sufferance *noun* a situation in which a previously lawful tenant is still in possession of property after the termination of the lease

tenancy at will *noun* a situation in which the owner of a property allows a tenant to occupy it as long as either party wishes

Tenancy Deposit Scheme for Regulated Agents *noun* a service that adjudicates on disputes about tenancy deposits at the end of a tenancy. Abbreviation **TDSRA**

tenancy in common *noun* a situation in which two or more persons jointly lease a property and each can leave his or her interest to an heir on death

tenant *noun* **1.** someone who rents a building, house, set of rooms, plot of land, or other piece of property for a fixed period of time **2.** someone living in or on a property ■ *verb* to live in or on someone else's property as a tenant

tenant at sufferance *noun* a tenant who continues to occupy a property after being told by the landlord to vacate it

tenant at will *noun* a tenant who holds a property at the will of the owner

tenant for life *noun* someone who can occupy a property for life

tenant for years *noun* a tenant who has been so for a period of several years and who has certain rights by law

tenant from year to year *noun* a tenant whose tenancy can be terminated only by a notice to quit on the anniversary of the tenancy

tenants in common *plural noun* the status of two or more owners of property who elect each to own a defined share of the asset, rather than owning the whole asset jointly

tenement *noun* **1.** property that is held by a tenant **2.** (*in Scotland*) a low-rise building of flats divided into sections each of which is served by a separate stair, especially one in an urban setting built in the early 20th century

Tenement Management Scheme *noun* a scheme, introduced by the Tenements (Scotland) Act 2004, that places obligations on owners of tenement flats in respect of the maintenance of certain parts of the tenement, most commonly those that should be maintained jointly

Tenements (Scotland) Act 2004 *noun* a piece of legislation that relates to tenement buildings and covers such issues as boundaries, the Tenement Management Scheme, dispute resolution, repairs and demolition

tenon *noun* a projection on one piece of wood or stone that fits into a matching recess (a mortice) on another piece so as to make a joint

tenure *noun* the right to hold property or a position

term *noun* the point at which a contract or agreement ends

termite infestation *noun* infestation of the timbers of a property by termites, which, over a period of years, can result in structural damage

terms and conditions of purchase *noun* a document detailing any special conditions that the purchaser of property attaches to the purchase

terms and conditions of sale *noun* a document detailing any special conditions that the seller of property attaches to the sale

terrace *noun* **1.** a long row of houses built together in the same style, separated only by shared dividing side walls **2.** a row of houses facing down from a raised position on or along the top of a piece of sloping ground, or built on a raised bank of ground **3.** a raised bank of ground, artificially constructed **4.** a promenade or portico, usually with columns or a balustrade along the side or sides ■ *verb* to convert land into a terrace or terraces

terracing *noun* **1.** a group of buildings designed or built as a terrace or series of terraces **2.** something built in shallow, gradually rising steps or tiers, e.g. open-air terraces in a football ground or an area of landscaped garden **3.** the act or process of creating a terrace or terraces

terracing effect *noun* a terrace structure effectively created by a new building erected between existing ones

territorial *adjective* relating to owned land

territory *noun* an area of land over which a government has control

thatch *noun* **1.** a plant material used as roofing on a house, e.g. straw or rushes. Also called **thatching 2.** a roof made of thatch ■ *verb* to put a roof of thatch on a building, or work at doing this

thatching *noun* **1.** the craft or process of constructing or repairing thatched roofs **2.** same as **thatch**

the Guild *abbreviation* National Guild of Removers and Storers

thermal insulation *noun* the act of insulating an object for the purpose of preventing heat from escaping from it or for preventing cold air from affecting it adversely

thermostat *noun* a device that regulates temperature by means of a temperature sensor, used, e.g., in domestic heating systems

thermostatic radiator valve *noun* a radiator valve containing a thermostat that operates the radiator according to the level set by the user on the valve itself. Abbreviation **TRV**

third party insurance *noun* insurance that pays compensation if someone who is not the insured person incurs loss or injury

thread *noun* the continuous helical ridge on a screw or pipe

three-core flex *noun* a type of electrical flex that contains live, neutral and earth wires, used for appliances that must be earthed

threshold *noun* **1.** a piece of stone or hardwood that forms the bottom of a doorway **2.** a doorway or entrance

throw up *verb* to erect a building or structure quickly

thumbscrew *noun* a screw with a flat head to be turned with the thumb and forefinger

tie *noun* **1.** a connecting, strengthening or supporting beam or rod **2.** either of two measurements on a survey line used to fix the position of a reference point

tie-in period *noun* a period for which a borrower agrees not to switch to a new mortgage lender, usually in return for a discounted interest rate

tie up *verb* **1.** to invest money in such a way that it cannot be used for other purposes **2.** to place legal restrictions on the selling or alienation of property

tile *noun* **1.** a thin flat or curved piece of baked, sometimes glazed, clay or synthetic material used to cover roofs, floors and walls, or for decoration **2.** a short pipe of baked clay, concrete or plastic used in making a drain **3.** *US* a hollow block of baked clay, concrete or gypsum used as a building material for walls or floors **4.** tiles considered collectively

tiler *noun* a contractor who lays tiles

tile spacer *noun* a small plastic stick or cross used when laying tiles to keep tiles evenly spaced, removed before grouting

tiling *noun* **1.** tiles that have been laid **2.** the laying of tiles on a roof, wall or floor **3.** tiles collectively

timber *noun* **1.** wood that has been sawn into boards, planks or other materials for use in building, woodworking or cabinetmaking **2.** a large piece of wood, usually squared, used in a building, e.g. as a beam

timbered *adjective* made of timber, or having exposed timbers

timber frame *noun* a skeleton frame of timbers around which a building is constructed

timber frame construction *noun* a type of construction in which a timber frame forms the skeleton of a building

timber preservation *noun* protecting the timber components in a house's structure from decay caused by damp, mould and pests

time barring *noun* the practice of setting a time limit on something, e.g. on the period during which claims may be made for the misselling of endowment policies

timeshare *noun* a property, usually an apartment in a resort area, that is jointly owned by people who use it at different times

Timeshare Consumers' Association *noun* a UK association that gives help and advice to timeshare owners on how to resolve a problem with a timeshare

tingle plate *noun* a thin wooden or plastic support for a bricklayer's line, to prevent it from sagging over long distances

tin mining search *noun* a check, conducted on behalf of a prospective purchaser, for evidence of tin mining in the area of the house, which may lead to concerns over subsidence

title *noun* **1.** the right to hold goods or property **2.** a document proving a right to hold a property

title deed, title document *noun* a document showing who owns a property

title guarantee *noun* same as **full title guarantee**

title insurance agent *noun US* a person who conducts the conveyancing process

title insurance company *noun US* a company that conducts the conveyancing process

title number *noun* a unique number assigned to a property by the Land Registry

title search *noun* an investigation, carried out by a conveyancer or solicitor, into the history of ownership of a property, checking for liens, unpaid claims, restrictions or any other problems that may affect ownership

titre *noun* (*in France*) a title deed

toe *verb* **1.** to drive in a nail or spike at an angle **2.** to fasten something with a nail or spike driven in at an angle

toenail *noun* a nail driven in at an angle, e.g. to join intersecting structural parts ■ *verb* to join parts of a structure with nails driven in at an angle

tolerance *noun* an allowance made for something to deviate in size from a standard, or the limit within which it is allowed to deviate

tongue and groove *noun* a type of joint between planks in which a projecting ridge on the edge of one plank fits into a groove on the edge of another

topcoat *noun* a finishing coat of paint, applied over an undercoat

topography *noun* the study and mapping of the features on the surface of land, including natural features such as mountains and rivers and constructed features such as roads and railways

topsoil *noun* the upper fertile layer of soil, from which plant roots take nutrients

top-up loan *noun* an additional loan offered to an existing mortgage customer at the same rate as the initial home loan

tower *noun* **1.** a tall structure, sometimes the upper part or a tall part of a building or structure and sometimes a separate building **2.** a tall scaffolding structure used in construction

Town and Country Planning Act *noun* a piece of UK legislation that consolidated the need for development to be subject to local-authority permission

town planner *noun* a person who supervises the design of a town, the way the streets and buildings in a town are laid out and how the land in a town used

town planning *noun* the activity of supervising the design of a town and the use of land in a town

tracker mortgage *noun* any mortgage with an interest rate that changes according to changes in another specified rate, usually the Bank of England base rate

trade association *noun* a group that joins together companies in the same type of business

trade fixtures *plural noun* equipment attached to a property by a tenant so that he or she can carry on a trade, which may be removed at the end of the tenancy

trade park *noun* an area in which several companies have factories or other commercial premises, typically in an out-of-town location

tradesman *noun* a man who works in a skilled trade, especially one related to the building trade, e.g. plumbing or carpentry

tradesperson *noun* someone who works in a skilled trade, especially one related to the building trade, e.g. plumbing or carpentry

traditional build construction *noun* same as **brick and block construction**

traffic schemes *plural noun* plans for the management of road traffic that form part of a local transport plan

transaction *noun* an instance of doing business of some kind, e.g. the purchase of a property

transaction date *noun* the date on which ownership of a property passes from the seller to the buyer

TransAction Protocol *noun* a national protocol introduced by the Law Society that standardised the procedures relating to conveyancing for domestic properties

transfer deed *noun* a document that transfers ownership of property

transferee *noun* someone to whom property or goods are transferred

transfer of title *noun* the transfer of ownership of property

transferor *noun* someone who transfers goods or property to another

transformer *noun* a device that transfers electrical energy from one alternating circuit to another with a change in voltage or current

transom *noun* **1.** a horizontal beam or stone above a window that supports the structure above **2.** a crosspiece over a door or between the top of a door and a window above **3.** a crossbar of wood or stone that divides a window horizontally

trave *noun* **1.** same as **crossbeam 2.** a section of a building formed by crossbeams, e.g. in a ceiling

traverse *noun* **1.** something that is fixed across a gap or lies crosswise, e.g. a structural member of a building **2.** a gallery or loft that crosses from side to side inside a building **3.** a railing, curtain, screen or partition forming a barrier within a building **4.** a survey made using a series of intersecting straight lines of known length whose angles of intersection are measured for recording on a map or in a table of data

tread *noun* **1.** the horizontal part of a step in a staircase **2.** the width of the horizontal part of a step, measured from front to back

tree preservation order *noun* an order from a local government department that prevents a tree from being cut down. Abbreviation **TPO**

tree surgeon *noun* a person who specialises in the treatment of diseased or old trees, by cutting or lopping branches

trellis *noun* a lattice of wood, metal or plastic used to support plants, usually fixed to a wall

trespass *noun* the offence of interfering with the land or goods of another person ■ *verb* to offend by going on to property without the permission of the owner

trespasser *noun* someone who commits trespass by going onto land without the permission of the owner

trestle *noun* **1.** a supporting framework consisting of a horizontal beam held up by a pair of splayed legs at each end **2.** a tower with sloping sides braced by horizontal crosspieces, used for supporting a bridge, made of timber, steel or reinforced concrete **3.** a bridge consisting of multiple short spans supported by towers with sloping sides braced by horizontal crosspieces

trowel *noun* a small hand tool with a short handle and a flat, usually pointed blade used for spreading, shaping and smoothing plaster, cement or mortar

trunking *noun* a casing used to anchor, conceal and protect cables and small pipes

truss *noun* an engineered load-bearing network of beams and bars used in the construction of a roof or other structure ■ *verb* to support or strengthen a roof, bridge or other elevated structure with a truss

trussed roof *noun* a roof constructed from prefabricated roof trusses

trust *noun* **1.** the duty of looking after goods, money or property that someone has passed to you **2.** the management of money or property for someone

trust deed *noun* a document that sets out the details of a trust

trustee *noun* a person who has charge of money or property in trust

Trustee Act 1925 *noun* a piece of UK legislation that consolidated certain previous enactments relating to trustees in England and Wales

trusteeship *noun* the position of being a trustee

TRV *abbreviation* thermostatic radiator valve

turpentine *noun* a colourless petroleum-based liquid used as a thinner for paint and varnish

turps *noun* turpentine (*informal*)

TVA *abbreviation* taxe sur la valeur

two-core flex *noun* a type of electrical flex that contains live and neutral wires but no earth wire, used for appliances that are not earthed

two tier lease *noun* a type of lease that applies to flats in blocks on housing estates

U

ufficio dell'agenzia del territorio *noun* (*in Italy*) the local land registry

ufficio imposte diretto *noun* (*in Italy*) a local tax office

UK Timber Frame Association *noun* a trade association for UK timber frame manufacturers and the key suppliers

unauthorised development *noun* any development for which local authority planning permission has not been granted

uncleared funds *noun* a payment made by cheque or electronic transfer, which must be verified by the bank and may fail if there are insufficient funds in the payer's account (NOTE: The process of clearing payments made in this way usually takes 3 working days.)

unconditional offer *noun* (*in Scotland*) an offer to buy property with no conditions or provisions attached

undercoat *noun* **1.** a coat of paint or emulsion applied to a surface before a top coat is applied **2.** paint or emulsion designed to be used as an undercoat

underfloor heating *noun* any of various room-heating systems installed under the floors

underlay *noun* a layer of cushioning and insulating material put down on a floor before a carpet is laid

underlet *verb* to let a property that is held on a lease

undermount sink *noun* a type of fitted sink in which the basin is set into the worktop

under offer *adjective* used for describing a property for sale on which an offer to buy has been submitted but the transaction has not yet been completed

underpin *verb* to support a weakened wall or structure by propping it up from below

underpinning *noun* a structure built to support a weakened wall or building

undertenant *noun* someone who holds a property on an underlease

undue influence *noun* wrongful pressure put on someone that prevents that person from acting independently

unexpired lease *noun* a lease that has not yet reached its term

Unfair Terms in Consumer Contracts Regulations 1999 *noun* a piece of UK legislation that protects consumers against unfair standard terms in contracts they make with traders

unfurnished *adjective* not furnished, or available to be rented without furniture

unimproved *adjective* used for describing land that is not modified in a way that would increase value, e.g. by the addition of buildings

unitary authority *noun* an administrative body responsible for the provision of all local government services in its area

unit holder *noun* an individual owner of a property in a set of properties that form a commonhold

unit-linked policy *noun* a life assurance policy in which a portion of the premium is used to buy life cover and the balance is invested in unit trusts

unplasticised polyvinyl chloride *noun* full form of **uPVC**

unplumbed *adjective* having no plumbing or sanitation installed

unprimed *adjective* not prepared for painting by the application of an undercoat or sealant

unsecured loan *noun* a loan made with no security

unsound *adjective* in a structurally poor or dangerous state

uplighter *noun* any light or light fitting designed to cast its light upwards

upstairs *adverb* to, towards or on an upper floor or level in a building ■ *noun* an upper floor or the part of a building above the ground floor

uPVC *noun* a type of tough synthetic material widely used in the construction industry, typically in the manufacture of window frames and doors. Full form **unplasticised polyvinyl chloride**

urbanización *noun* (*in Spain*) a number of properties, typically holiday homes, arranged into an estate

urban regeneration *noun* measures taken to improve the quality of the built environment in urban areas regarded as being in need of development and improvement

urban regeneration company *noun* a partnership of representatives from the public and private sectors who aim to deliver physical and economic regeneration in specific areas

use *noun* land held by the legal owner on trust for a beneficiary (NOTE: The use of a property can govern what rates are payable, such as council tax or business rates.)

usufruct *noun* the right to enjoy the use or the profit of the property or land of another person

utilities *plural noun* services such as water, gas and electricity

utility bill *noun* a bill for a service such as water, gas or electricity

utility company *noun* a company that provides a service such as water, gas or electricity

V

vacant possession *noun* the right to occupy a property immediately after buying it because it is empty

vacating receipt *noun* a document provided by a mortgage lender to certify that all money owed to it in respect of the property has been paid

valuation *noun* **1.** the act of determining the value or price of something, especially property **2.** the price of something established by appraisal of its quality, condition and desirability, or of the cost of replacement

valuation for mortgage purposes *noun* a brief survey of a property, sent to a mortgage lender, that comments on its value only and makes no comment on its structural soundness

Valuation Office Agency *noun* an executive agency of HM Revenue & Customs with various functions in relation to the valuation of property in the UK

valuation surveyor *noun* a surveyor who carries out valuations for mortgage purposes

valuation tribunal *noun* a tribunal that settles disputes relating to non-domestic rates and council tax set by a local authority

value *noun* **1.** an amount expressed in money or another medium of exchange that is thought to be a fair exchange for something **2.** the worth, importance or usefulness of something to someone ■ *verb* to estimate or determine the value of something such as a property

value-added tax *noun* full form of **VAT**

valuer *noun* someone who values property for insurance purposes

vanity *noun* US a cabinet that holds a sink and its plumbing, usually with drawers or shelves under the sink for storage

vapour barrier *noun* a protective barrier, usually of polythene or foil-backed plasterboard, designed to prevent the passage of moisture through a structure, usually a wall, thereby eliminating its condensation on cooler surfaces behind

variable rate *noun* a rate of interest on a loan that is not fixed but can change with the current bank interest rates. Also called **floating rate**

variable-rate mortgage *noun* a mortgage on which interest is payable at a rate that changes, usually in accordance with market interest rates

VAT *noun* a tax on the increased value of a product or service added at each stage of its production or distribution, paid by the consumer. Full form **value-added tax**

Velux a trade name for a type of window designed to be set into a pitched roof

vendee *noun* someone who buys something

vendor *noun* the person who is selling something

veneer *noun* **1.** a thin layer of a material bonded to the surface of a less attractive or inferior material **2.** an outer layer applied to a surface for decoration or protection, e.g. a facing of stone on a brick building **3.** a thin layer of wood that is glued together with others to make plywood

Venetian blind *noun* a window blind consisting of narrow slats, which can be tilted to allow light through without raising the blind

vente en l'état futur d'achèvement *noun* (*in France*) the sale of an unfinished property

ventilation *noun* the means of supplying fresh air to an enclosed space, e.g. an opening or a piece of equipment installed in a building

veranda *noun* a porch, usually roofed and sometimes partly enclosed, that extends along an outside wall of a building

verge *noun* **1.** a narrow border that runs alongside a road **2.** the edge of a sloping roof where it extends beyond the gable

verification of employment *noun* written confirmation of the employment status of someone applying for a mortgage, usually required by the lender before funds are released

vernacular *noun* the local architecture of a place or people, especially the architectural style that is used for ordinary houses as opposed to large official or commercial buildings

vernacular building *noun* a building built in the distinctive local style of the place where it is found

vertical blind *noun* a window blind which is opened at one side of the window rather than raised to the top

vest *verb* to transfer to someone the legal ownership and possession of land or of a right

vested *adjective* having an unquestionable right to the possession of property or a privilege

vested interest *noun* an interest in a property that will come into a person's possession when the interest of another person ends

vestibule *noun* a small room or hall between an outer door and the main part of a building

vesting assent *noun* a document that vests settled land on a tenant for life

vesting order *noun* a court order that transfers property

vibration white finger *noun* a medical complaint caused by frequent use of hand-held vibrating tools such as pneumatic drills

vices apparents *plural noun* (*in France*) visible defects of a property

vices cachés *plural noun* (*in France*) hidden defects of a property

Victorian *adjective* in, or typical of, the elaborate style of architecture popular in Britain in the later 19th century

view *noun* a scene or an area that can be seen, especially one that is pleasing or impressive ■ *verb* to visit a property that you are thinking of renting or buying

viewer *noun* someone visiting a property who is interested in buying or renting it, or who is officially inspecting it

viewing *noun* an act of looking at or inspecting a property with a view to buying it

villa *noun* **1.** a large luxurious house in the country **2.** a detached or semidetached house in a residential area built in the late 19th or early 20th century (*dated*) **3.** (*in New Zealand*) a detached suburban house built in the late 19th or early 20th century, usually with a veranda and bay window

vinyl *noun* a wipe-clean flooring material made from a type of plastic, used in areas such as kitchens and bathrooms

visual inspection *noun* a relatively superficial inspection of such things as electrical and gas systems in a property, carried out as part of a general survey, as distinct from any detailed inspection carried out as part of a specialist survey

voltage *noun* an electrical force measured in volts

voluntary disposition *noun* the transfer of property without any valuable consideration

Voluntary Purchase Scheme *noun* a government scheme under which tenants of registered social landlords may be able to apply to buy the home they rent at a discount

W

wainscot *noun* **1.** a lining for the walls of a room, especially one made of wood panelling. Also called **wainscoting 2.** the lower part of the wall of a room, especially when it is panelled in wood or finished differently from the upper part **3.** a fine grade of oak used as wall panelling ■ *verb* to cover a wall with wood panelling

wainscoting *noun* **1.** the material, especially wood, used to cover a wall **2.** same as **wainscot**

wall *noun* **1.** a vertical structure forming an inside partition or an outside surface of a building **2.** a narrow upright structure, usually built of stone, wood, plaster or brick, that acts as a boundary or keeps something in or out ■ *verb* to close an opening with a wall

wall fittings *plural noun* fittings such as shelves and mirrors that are fixed to walls

wall insulation *noun* any of various forms of insulation added either to the surface of a wall or to the cavity between the skins of a cavity wall

wall light *noun* a light fitting fixed to a wall

wallpaper *noun* paper, usually printed with a pattern, that is pasted on walls and sometimes ceilings as a covering and decoration

wallplate *noun* a horizontal structural member placed along the top of a wall to support the ends of beams, joists or trusses

wall stitching *noun* the use of grouted anchors that hold together the outer and inner leaves of a rubble-filled wall

wall tie *noun* any of various devices used for securing a structural member to a wall or for tying the two skins of a cavity wall together

wall tile *noun* a ceramic tile, often decorative, used to make surfaces waterproof and easy to clean in a bathroom or kitchen

wall unit *noun* a shelving unit that fits onto or against a wall

warehouse apartment *noun* a large, typically open-plan apartment created when a large commercial or industrial property such as a warehouse or a factory is converted for residential purposes

warrantor *noun* someone who gives a warranty

warranty *noun* **1.** a guarantee on purchased goods that they are of the quality represented and will be replaced or repaired if found to be faulty **2.** a condition in an insurance contract in which the insured person guarantees that something is the case **3.** a covenant guaranteeing the security of the title to property being sold

washer *noun* **1.** a small disc or ring used to keep a screw or bolt secure or prevent leakage at a joint **2.** an appliance used for washing, especially a washing machine

washer dryer *noun* a machine that both washes and dries clothes

waste *noun* **1.** unwanted or unusable items, remains, by-products or household rubbish **2.** used or contaminated water from domestic, industrial, or mining applications **3.** loss of value in a property or estate caused by damage done by the tenant

waste collection authority *noun* a local authority in its role as the collector of domestic and business waste in a district or region

water closet *noun* full form of **WC**

water damage *noun* damage to the fabric and contents of a property caused by water

water drainage search *noun* a check of a property, conducted on behalf of a prospective purchaser, to establish various pieces of information in relation to water drainage, e.g. whether the property is connected to a public sewer

Water Industry Commission for Scotland *noun* the regulator of the water industry in Scotland

water meter *noun* a device that records the amount of water that passes through a pipe, usually for billing purposes

water pressure *noun* the pressure of water in a system, e.g. a mains system or a gravity-fed central heating system

water regulations *plural noun* regulations that apply to the provision of water services

Water Regulations Advisory Scheme *noun* a scheme, fully funded by the UK water supply companies, established in order to assist consumers in finding to water installations that meet the requirements of the water regulations

water supply search *noun* a check of a property, conducted on behalf of a prospective purchaser, to establish various pieces of information in relation to water supply, e.g. whether the property is connected to a public or private water supply

water tank *noun* a storage tank for water, e.g. a cold storage tank in a gravity-fed domestic water system

Water UK *noun* the industry association that represents all UK water and waste water service suppliers at national and European level

waterways search *noun* a check of a property in close proximity to a waterway to establish ownership of the riverbanks, fishing rights, licences to abstract water and drainage rights

watt *noun* an SI unit of measurement of electrical power. The work done by an electrical circuit or the power consumed is measured in watts. Symbol **W**

WC *noun* a small room containing a toilet. Full form **water closet**

wealth tax *noun* a tax on money, property or investments owned by a person

weatherboard *noun* **1.** a sloping piece of wood fitted to the bottom of a door to allow rain to run off **2.** a grooved piece of timber used as part of a series of overlapping horizontal pieces forming cladding for walls or roofs ■ *verb* to fit a building with weatherboards

weathered *adjective* **1.** worn, damaged or seasoned by exposure to the weather **2.** given an artificial appearance of having been exposed to weather **3.** having a sloping surface so that rain can run off

weathering *noun* the effect of prolonged exposure to the weather

weatherproofing *noun* materials and methods used for making a property or structure weatherproof

web *noun* a ribbed surface within a vaulted structure such as an I-beam

welder *noun* someone whose job involves the fusion of pieces or parts of a particular material using heat or pressure

wet room *noun* a bathroom with a sealed floor and an open shower area from which water flows into a drain set into the floor

white goods *plural noun* major electrical household appliances such as fridges, freezers and microwave ovens

white land *noun* land between an urban area and green belt that may be required to meet longer-term development needs

whole of life policy *noun* an insurance policy for which a insured person continues to pay premiums for the rest of his or her life, as distinct from a policy that provides life cover for a fixed term only and does not pay out if the insured person does not die within the term

wildlife corridor *noun* a set of near-adjacent wildlife habitats formed into a single strip for conservation purposes

wind damage *noun* damage to property caused by high winds

windfall land *noun* land that becomes available to a local authority for development as a result of a demolition

wind farm, wind park *noun* a group of large windmills or wind turbines, built to harness the wind to produce electricity

window seat *noun* an indoor seat fixed to a wall under a window, especially a window that is set into a recess

wire cutters *plural noun* a heavy-duty hand tool with blades for cutting through wire

wire strippers *plural noun* a hand tool used for stripping the plastic insulation from electrical wire

wiring *noun* **1.** a network of electrical wires **2.** the act or process of installing a system of electrical wires

with-profits policy *noun* a savings plan, often an endowment linked to a mortgage, in which money is invested in a mix of shares, property and bonds, with bonuses added each year and a larger terminal bonus added when the policy matures

witness *noun* someone who signs a document to show that it, or another signature, is genuine

woodblock *noun* a small flat piece of wood laid in a pattern with others to make a floor surface

wood boring beetle *noun* any of various species of beetle whose larvae or adult forms eat and thereby destroy wood

woodchip *noun* chips of wood used as a surfacing material, e.g. on paths and children's playgrounds

woodwork *noun* **1.** the skill or craft of making items out of wood **2.** items or components made from wood, especially the interior parts of a building, e.g. the frames of windows, staircases and doors

woodworm *noun* the damaged condition of wood from its infestation by wood-boring insects, especially larvae

working day *noun* a day on which people work, usually, but not always, a weekday

working from home *noun* a way of working in which employees work at home, usually on a computer, and send the finished work back to the employer's office (NOTE: Business rates may be payable if a person's domestic property is used for home working.)

wraparound loan *noun* a loan that permits an existing loan to be refinanced at an interest rate between the original loan rate and the currently prevailing market rate

wrench *noun* 1. *US* same as **spanner 2.** a spanner, especially a large one, with adjustable jaws

written offer *noun* (*in Scotland*) a written offer to purchase a property, usually submitted after a verbal offer has been made

YZ

Yale lock a trade name for a cylinder lock often used on the front doors of residential properties

yield *noun* a return on an investment in the form of interest or dividends ■ *verb* to gain an amount as a return on an investment

zoning *noun* an order by a local council that land shall be used only for one type of building

Zurich Municipal Newbuild scheme *noun* a warranty scheme, similar to the NHBC scheme, for newly built properties

Zurich Municipal Rebuild scheme *noun* a warranty scheme, similar to the NHBC scheme, for rebuilt properties

SUPPLEMENTS

Buying a House - The 12-Step Process
Snagging List
Sales Particulars Template
Home Information Pack
Questions to Ask your Estate Agent
Property Statistics for the UK
Property Misdescriptions Act 1991
Buying Abroad - Top 20 European Destinations

Buying a House - The 12-Step Process

1. Set budget
Decide what you can afford to spend on a property based on your income, using a mortgage calculator or the advice of a mortgage advisor.

2. Find a property
Get house-hunting!

3. Make an offer
This is when should name the price that you are willing to pay for your chosen property, either verbally or in writing to the estate agent. At this stage you can negotiate with the seller to reduce the price.

4. Agreement in principle
This is a preliminary agreement from a mortgage lender that, all being well, they will lend you the appropriate amount for a mortgage. It is not yet tied to the property in question.

5. Appoint a solicitor
At this stage you should have somebody in place to take care of the legal conveyancing.

6. Mortgage application
This is a full written application to the lender with regard to the property in question. Mortgage fees are also paid now.

7. Valuation/survey
The property is given a full inspection on behalf of the mortgage lender, anything from a standard valuation to a full structural survey for older or unusual properties.

8. Verification of identity/income
The mortgage lender will check your credit history, employment status and current address details.

9. Offer from mortgage lender
In response to the mortgage application and the valuation or survey, the lender will make a formal offer for the terms of the mortgage.

10. Draw up contracts
The solicitor is responsible for making a contract which all applicants must sign. The deposit is also paid at this stage.

11. Exchange of contracts
This is the point at which you are legally obliged to continue with the purchase.

12. Completion
The final stage, this is the day on which you take possession of the property and move in. Enjoy your new home!

Snagging List

This list gives a basic idea of what a purchaser should be looking for when checking a new property. It may be helpful to compile a checklist of faults for each room, which can then be passed on to a builder or property developer.

BASIC CHECKS - to be carried out in every room (including hallways and staircases)

Ceilings -
- Inspect coving fittings
- Check for discoloration, cracking or bulging

Doors -
- Check condition of frame
- Are they the correct size and properly hung?
- Can they be easily opened and closed?
- Do the locks (if any) work? Are the keys supplied?

Fixtures/Fittings -
- Light switches - do they work?
- Inspect switch fittings
- Inspect light fittings
- Fireplaces - are they functional? Are the chimneys clear?
- Inspect fireplace fittings
- Power points - do they work?
- Inspect power point fittings

Floors -
- Check installation of floor fittings
- Check condition of carpets / floorboards

Furnishings -
- Check condition of furnishings
- Check DIY fittings (e.g. picture hangings, shelves, television mountings)
- Inspect furnishings for fire safety compliance

General -
- Is the paintwork even? Is it chipped or scratched?
- Check that fittings are consistent and matching
- Check for damage caused by removed fittings

Snagging List *cont.*

Walls -
- Check for discoloration, cracking or bulging
- Inspect skirting board fittings
- Are tiles properly fitted and hygienic?

Windows -
- Can they be easily opened and closed?
- Do the locks (if any) work? Are the keys supplied?

KITCHEN CHECKS

Appliances -
- Does the dishwasher work?
- Does the oven work?
- Do the hobs work?
- Does the fridge/freezer work?
- Does the washing machine work?

Fixtures/Fittings -
- Check extractor fan (if any). Is there enough ventilation?
- Do the taps work?
- Check that drawers open and close easily
- Inspect sink fitting, including underneath
- Inspect worktop installation and condition

BATHROOM CHECKS - including en suites and separate washrooms

Fixtures/Fittings -
- Inspect shower fitting
- Inspect bath and bath panel fitting
- Inspect sink fitting, including underneath
- Do the taps work? (check both bath and basin)
- Check that toilet functions correctly
- Check bidet (if any)
- Check extractor fan (if any)

EXTERNAL CHECKS

Doors -
- Check condition of frames
- Are they the correct size and properly hung?
- Can they be easily opened and closed?
- Do the locks work? Are the keys supplied?
- Check for other security measures, such as chains / peepholes
- Are they fitted with deadbolts?

Other -
- Inspect gates and fencing
- Check condition of paths
- Inspect garden features including patio fitting
- Inspect brickwork and pointing
- Is the roof in good condition?
- Can the garage door be easily opened and closed?
- Does the garage door lock work? Are the keys supplied?
- Check external tap(s)
- Check external light fittings and switches

OTHER CHECKS

Utilities -
- Locate and check water meter, and take reading
- Locate stopcock
- Locate and check gas meter, and take reading
- Locate and check electricity meter, and take reading

Other -
- Inspect boiler
- Inspect radiators / other heating system
- Inspect air conditioning system (if any)
- Is there a thermostat? Is it working?
- How is the loft (if any) accessed?
- Does the under-stairs cupboard door open and close easily?
- Inspect stairs and banisters
- Is there a smoke alarm fitted? Does it work?
- Is there a burglar alarm system fitted? Does it work?
- Is there a clear exit route in case of emergency?

Sales Particulars Template

ADDRESS OF PROPERTY

Introduction –

Synopsis of property details highlighting the most desirable points

Situation –

General description of where the property is situated, including nearby towns

Communications –

Details of road, rail and air links

Schools –

Details of nearby primary, secondary and private schools

Leisure –

Nearby sports, entertainment and leisure facilities

Directions –

Description of how best to access the property

Tenure –

Type and length of contract and date of possession

Description –

Paragraph of property details including number of bedrooms, utilities and any stand-out characteristics

Accommodation –

Room-by-room description, giving room dimensions, a basic description of fixtures and fittings, and pointing out any especially desirable features

Also describes storage, corridor and stairway areas, gardens and parking (if any)

General remarks / stipulations –

Including the following: utility providers, details of council tax, useful addresses, details of acting solicitor and building manager (if any) and any small print limiting estate agent's liability.

To arrange a viewing –

Estate agent's details.

FLOOR PLAN - *appendix*

Home Information Pack

Required documents:

An index (a list of the contents of the Pack)
A sale statement (summarising terms of sale)
Evidence of title
Standard searches (i.e. local authority enquiries and a drainage and water search)
An energy performance certificate
Where appropriate, commonhold information (including a copy of the commonhold community statement)
Where appropriate, leasehold information (including a copy of the lease, information on service charges and insurance)
Where appropriate, a new home warranty
Where appropriate, a report on a home that is not physically complete
A home condition report*

Authorised documents:

Guarantees and warranties
Other searches

* The Regulations will be amended so that as from 1 June 2007 the home condition report will be an authorised part of the Pack.

Information from the Department for Communities and Local Government
www.homeinformationpacks.gov.uk

Questions to Ask your Estate Agent

Why is the owner selling?
If you find that the owner needs to have the money quickly or is otherwise keen for a quick sale, you may be able to make a lower offer.

How long has the property been on the market?
If the property has been unsold for a long time, this may indicate a hidden problem. Alternatively, it may mean that the seller will be prepared to accept a lower offer.

When does the current owner/occupier need to move out?
If you can meet an urgent deadline and reduce stress for the seller by allowing them to sort things out promptly, it might be an advantage in negotiations. You may also be in a stronger position if you can arrange for the property to be occupied promptly if a current tenant is moving out

What is the minimum price the seller will accept?
If a property has been on the market a while, it's quite likely that the seller will accept less. An estate agent should be able to give an indication so you can formulate your offer.

What do you think the property will actually sell for?
This question should give an indication of whether the estate agent has any concerns about the price asked for the property. If they think it has been overvalued, they might be able to persuade the seller of this.

Who priced the property?
A question following on from the previous on: if the estate agent themselves valued the property, they're likely to push for a close offer. If the seller put a price on it, as before, the estate agent may be able to persuade them to accept a lower price.

Are there any similar properties on the market?
Knowing what the current market is like will help you to formulate an offer. However, the estate agent is not likely to volunteer the information when this may compromise the deal they are trying to close! You may get more of an indication by looking around at what other companies have on their books.

What comes with the property?
Some sellers will want to leave inconvenient items of furniture, some will want to take everything from the lightbulbs to the door handles and the shelves from the walls. It's helpful to know what you can expect on moving-in day – you may also find some hidden extras.

Property Statistics for the UK

Overall average house prices:

Detached: £300,349
Semi-detached: £180,170
Terrace: £158,493
Flat: £185,703

Average price: £199,184
Annual % rise: 7.71%

Average house prices by region:

	Detached	Semi-detached	Terrace	Flat	**Average price**	Average % rise
Greater London	£601,214	£348,620	£336,077	£270,146	**£317,790**	8.3%
South East	£382,696	£222,085	£184,071	£155,727	**£236,915**	6.1%
South West	£301,790	£188,322	£165,414	£150,883	**£205,768**	5.3%
East Anglia	£271,396	£160,274	£142,649	£134,534	**£181,925**	4%
West Midlands	£270,804	£151,385	£123,309	£129,141	**£164,576**	6.1%
East Midlands	£247,938	£151,152	£113,922	£128,204	**£156,243**	4.4%
Northern Ireland	£243,987	£139,726	£120,510	£124,814	**£153,868**	25.4%
Wales	£237,749	£138,671	£109,538	£124,409	**£149,058**	7.8%
Yorks and Humber	£237,482	£140,046	£108,928	£121,403	**£147,230**	10.1%
North-West	£227,485	No data	£101,075	£113,996	**£146,601**	11%
North	£221,836	£137,286	£105,225	£111,464	**£137,861**	-39.3%
Scotland	No data	No data	No data	No data	**£130,681**	11.1%

Data from the Land Register of England and Wales. Figures are for the period May 2005-April 2006.

Property Statistics for the UK *cont.*

Top 15 highest-priced areas:

	Detached	Semi-detached	Terrace	Flat	**Average price**	Annual % rise
Windsor and Maidenhead	£521,715	£299,929	£297,228	£229,477	**£350,590**	6%
Surrey	£553,220	£282,184	£242,144	£196,862	**£330,966**	9.9%
Greater London	£601,214	£348,620	£336,077	£270,146	**£317,790**	8.3%
Buckinghamshire	£487,467	£249,163	£202,068	£169,894	**£314,035**	10.6%
Wokingham	£390,754	£243,737	£210,677	£191,148	**£283,996**	7.8%
Hertfordshire	£487,569	£275,312	£215,269	£164,714	**£268,095**	7.1%
Oxfordshire	£393,281	£230,196	£208,259	£187,995	**£260,353**	8.3%
Poole	£347,386	£195,493	£183,202	£221,652	**£256,011**	3.8%
West Berkshire	£365,135	£225,199	£197,203	£174,824	**£254,43**	0.8%
Bath / North-East Somerset	£379,441	£233,410	£210,371	£202,783	**£251,444**	5.7%
Hampshire	£357,315	£212,678	£178,329	£148,208	**£239,300**	4.8%
Dorset	£320,640	£216,904	£185,780	£152,598	**£238,911**	6.3%
Rutland	£303,141	£168,121	£165,159	£136,099	**£237,906**	5.3%
West Sussex	£358,322	£226,475	£187,752	£148,282	**£233,839**	2.9%
Brighton and Hove	£420,268	£257,319	£251,987	£180,144	**£231,957**	6.1%

Data from the Land Register of England and Wales. Figures are for the period May 2005-April 2006.

Property Misdescriptions Act 1991

An Act to prohibit the making of false or misleading statements about property matters in the course of estate agency business and property development business.

1.— (1) Where a false or misleading statement about a prescribed matter is made in the course of an estate agency business or a property development business, otherwise than in providing conveyancing services, the person by whom the business is carried on shall be guilty of an offence under this section.

(2) Where the making of the statement is due to the act or default of an employee the employee shall be guilty of an offence under this section; and the employee may be proceeded against and punished whether or not proceedings are also taken against his employer.

(3) A person guilty of an offence under this section shall be liable—
(a) on summary conviction, to a fine not exceeding the statutory maximum, and;
(b) on conviction on indictment, to a fine.

(4) No contract shall be void or unenforceable, and no right of action in civil proceedings in respect of any loss shall arise, by reason only of the commission of an offence under this section.

(5) For the purposes of this section—
(a) "false" means false to a material degree,
(b) a statement is misleading if (though not false) what a reasonable person may be expected to infer from it, or from any omission from it, is false,
(c) a statement may be made by pictures or any other method of signifying meaning as well as by words and, if made by words, may be made orally or in writing,
(d) a prescribed matter is any matter relating to land which is specified in an order made by the Secretary of State,
(e) a statement is made in the course of an estate agency business if (but only if) the making of the statement is a thing done as mentioned in subsection (1) of section 1 of the [1979 c. 38.] Estate Agents Act 1979 and that Act either applies to it or would apply to it but for subsection (2)(a) of that section,

(f) a statement is made in the course of a property development business if (but only if) it is made—

(i) in the course of a business (including a business in which the person making the statement is employed) concerned wholly or substantially with the development of land, and

(ii) for the purpose of, or with a view to, disposing of an interest in land consisting of or including a building, or a part of a building, constructed or renovated in the course of the business, and

(g) "conveyancing services" means the preparation of any transfer, conveyance, writ, contract or other document in connection with the disposal or acquisition of an interest in land, and services ancillary to that, but does not include anything done as mentioned in section 1(1)(a) of the Estate Agents Act 1979.

(6) For the purposes of this section any reference in this section or section 1 of the Estate Agents Act 1979 to disposing of or acquiring an interest in land—

(a) in England and Wales and Northern Ireland shall be construed in accordance with section 2 of that Act, and

(b) in Scotland is a reference to the transfer or creation of an "interest in land" as defined in section 28(1) of the [1979 c. 33.] Land Registration (Scotland) Act 1979.

(7) An order under this section may—

(a) make different provision for different cases, and

(b) include such supplemental, consequential and transitional provisions as the Secretary of State considers appropriate;

and the power to make such an order shall be exercisable by statutory instrument which shall be subject to annulment in pursuance of a resolution of either House of Parliament.

2.— (1) In proceedings against a person for an offence under section 1 above it shall be a defence for him to show that he took all reasonable steps and exercised all due diligence to avoid committing the offence.

(2) A person shall not be entitled to rely on the defence provided by subsection (1) above by reason of his reliance on information given by another unless he shows that it was reasonable in all the circumstances for him to have relied on the information, having regard in particular—

(a) to the steps which he took, and those which might reasonably have been taken, for the purpose of verifying the information, and

(b) to whether he had any reason to disbelieve the information.

(3) Where in any proceedings against a person for an offence under section 1 above the defence provided by subsection (1) above involves an allegation that the commission of the offence was due—

(a) to the act or default of another, or

(b) to reliance on information given by another,

the person shall not, without the leave of the court, be entitled to rely on the defence unless he has served a notice under subsection (4) below on the person bringing the proceedings not less than seven clear days before the hearing of the proceedings or, in Scotland, the diet of trial.

(4) A notice under this subsection shall give such information identifying or assisting in the identification of the person who committed the act or default, or gave the information, as is in the possession of the person serving the notice at the time he serves it.

3.— The Schedule to this Act (which makes provision about the enforcement of this Act) shall have effect.

4.— (1) Where an offence under this Act committed by a body corporate is proved to have been committed with the consent or connivance of, or to be attributable to neglect on the part of, a director, manager, secretary or other similar officer of the body corporate or a person who was purporting to act in such a capacity, he (as well as the body corporate) is guilty of the offence and liable to be proceeded against and punished accordingly.

(2) Where the affairs of a body corporate are managed by its members, subsection (1) above applies in relation to the acts and defaults of a member in connection with his functions of management as if he were a director of the body corporate.

(3) Where an offence under this Act committed in Scotland by a Scottish partnership is proved to have been committed with the consent or connivance of, or to be attributable to neglect on the part of, a partner, he (as well as the partnership) is guilty of the offence and liable to be proceeded against and punished accordingly.